Building Web Applications with ArcGIS

Build an engaging GIS Web application from scratch using ArcGIS

Hussein Nasser

BIRMINGHAM - MUMBAI

Building Web Applications with ArcGIS

First published: November 2014

Production reference: 1121114

Published by Packt Publishing Ltd.
Livery Place
35 Livery Street
Birmingham B3 2PB, UK.

ISBN 978-1-78355-295-5

www.packtpub.com

Credits

Author

Hussein Nasser

Reviewers

Hani M. Basheer

Brian Small

Commissioning Editor

Kunal Parikh

Acquisition Editor

Llewellyn Rozario

Content Development Editor

Rahul Nair

Technical Editors

Mrunmayee Patil

Aman Preet Singh

Copy Editors

Janbal Dharmaraj

Laxmi Subramanian

Project Coordinator

Judie Jose

Proofreaders

Ameesha Green

Amy Johnson

Indexers

Monica Ajmera Mehta

Tejal Soni

Production Coordinator

Nilesh R. Mohite

Cover Work

Nilesh R. Mohite

About the Author

Hussein Nasser is an Esri award-winning senior GIS solution architect at Electricity and Water Authority, Bahrain. He is the author of two books on ArcGIS, *Administering ArcGIS for Server* and *Learning ArcGIS Geodatabases*, both published by Packt Publishing. In 2007, Hussein won the first place in the annual ArcGIS Server Code Challenge conducted at the Esri Developer Summit in Palm Springs, California, for using AJAX technology with ArcGIS for Server, which was not implemented back then. After his 8-year career as a GIS Architect in the leading Middle Eastern Engineering company, Khatib & Alami, where he spent time implementing various utility GIS systems based on Esri technology across the Middle East, Hussein decided to move to a more focused environment in Electricity and Water Authority back in Bahrain, his homeland. Here he can channel his expertise to develop a robust GIS utility solution that is fully integrated with the eGovernment project, which will help Bahrain march towards the smart grid. Beyond GIS, Hussein is fascinated by acute research topics; some of the papers he is currently working on are *The Human API: A Software Interface to Prevent Cancer*, *Global Economic Crisis and Natural Disasters Quantum Detector*, and *Stock Market change with the Moon Phases*.

I would like to thank Nada; most of this book was written in our favorite coffee shop. You wouldn't be holding this book if she wasn't there.

About the Reviewers

Hani M. Basheer is a GIS expert, Oracle Certified Professional DBA, and Esri Certified ArcGIS Desktop Associate. He has graduated as a surveying engineer with a technical Postgraduate Diploma in Esri GIS. He has over 15 years of experience in the field of Geographic Information Systems (GIS) Esri products.

Throughout his career, he has worked on several enterprise GIS projects in Egypt and Saudi Arabia; he has also worked with the Egyptian SDI project. He moved to Saudi Arabia in 2007 to work with a leading GIS company, Farsi GeoTech, dealing with many GIS projects. Hani moved to National Water Company in 2010 to establish a GIS unit for managing water and waste water utilities networks in Jeddah city.

Hani has over 10 years of experience in the field of technical training for Esri GIS products. During this period, he has delivered many successful training sessions in the Middle East to different business industries such as petroleum, mining, education, electricity, and municipalities.

Throughout his career, he has worked with most of Esri products, ArcGIS, Geodatabase, ArcGIS Server, ArcSDE, Python, Arc Objects, and Esri extensions. He has also worked with Oracle RDBMSs, where he earned four DBA OCPs, and with SAN storage, GPS, and GPS CORS systems.

I really like this book! While I was reviewing it, I found it so interesting that I could not put it down. The writer has successfully transferred his knowledge in an easy and readable way. I can guarantee you will get the best knowledge required for your GIS career by reading this book.

I would like to thank my wife, Wegdan, for her love and support. I also wish to acknowledge my loving family who is always there for me.

Brian Small is a self-confessed computer geek since age 11 and has been in the field for nearly 30 years. He earned his first computer (a Franklin Ace 500) by picking raspberries and strawberries at his family's farm, and has learned coding by typing the listings from the Nibble and Byte magazines in the 1980s. His early IT career was focused on end-user technical support and dabbling with application development. His mid-IT career focused more on administration of enterprise business systems such as work management, inventory/purchasing management, and GIS systems. Currently, his main focus is on the administration of GIS systems based on the Esri product platform and developing web mapping applications.

Outside of work, his interests are diverse, which include playing the piano, wandering the trails and backpacking in the North Cascades, building a digital weaving loom, and building his own CNC machine.

Brian has worked in the local government for over 16 years providing IT and GIS support, which included providing end-user technical support, supervision of support technicians, administration of various enterprise systems, and also as a GIS senior analyst who administers ArcGIS for Server, ArcSDE, ArcGIS Online, and other Esri products as well as developing web mapping applications based on the Esri JavaScript API.

Currently, Brian is a partner in Salish Coast Sciences, LLC—a small company that provides GIS consulting services, which include GIS system evaluation, GIS system implementation, web application development, and so on.

I'd like to thank my "gramma" for buying me my first electronics kit for Christmas that piqued my interest in technology, my mom for encouraging me to excel in my studies at school, my dad for teaching me how to be like MacGyver to make/fix things out of a seemingly senseless pile of spare parts, my sister for being there to share in the mischief we caused, and all the other individuals I have crossed paths with who have influenced the person who I am today.

---

www.PacktPub.com

Support files, eBooks, discount offers, and more

For support files and downloads related to your book, please visit www.PacktPub.com.

Did you know that Packt offers eBook versions of every book published, with PDF and ePub files available? You can upgrade to the eBook version at www.PacktPub.com and as a print book customer, you are entitled to a discount on the eBook copy. Get in touch with us at service@packtpub.com for more details.

At www.PacktPub.com, you can also read a collection of free technical articles, sign up for a range of free newsletters and receive exclusive discounts and offers on Packt books and eBooks.

http://PacktLib.PacktPub.com

Do you need instant solutions to your IT questions? PacktLib is Packt's online digital book library. Here, you can search, access, and read Packt's entire library of books.

Why subscribe?

- Fully searchable across every book published by Packt
- Copy and paste, print, and bookmark content
- On demand and accessible via a web browser

Free access for Packt account holders

If you have an account with Packt at www.PacktPub.com, you can use this to access PacktLib today and view 9 entirely free books. Simply use your login credentials for immediate access.

Table of Contents

Preface

Building Web Applications with ArcGIS is a short book. Short books are hard to write, because I have to condense essential information into less than 150 pages. It is challenging to determine what is essential when you know a lot about a particular subject. The writer has to sacrifice of some content so that they can produce a quality title that readers can really benefit from.

ArcGIS is a suite of software, developed by Esri — Environmental Systems Research Institute. ArcGIS allows its users to view, edit, analyze, and work with geographic data. You can work with geographic data on desktop, web, or mobile. This book tackles the web development side of ArcGIS; it teaches the reader how to build web applications that can interact with ArcGIS.

I am very proud of this title. It is a special book because I have tried a new writing style I haven't used before. This is the first book I have ever written that is purely based on a real-life project. As a reader, you act like a web development company where your clients hand you their requirements. Chapter by chapter you start building the application required by the client gradually: adding functionalities, studying their feasibility, and implementing accordingly. Not only will this teach you the basics of developments for ArcGIS, but it will also relate to your real-life projects as well.

I get bored when I read a book that is cluttered with methods and functions and I have to figure out when and where to use them. Some books give you examples disconnected from reality that you won't ever encounter in your lifetime. This book is different, as each method you use, each library you add, contributes to a requirement requested by a client and it makes sense. You will read and say "yes, this is something my client would definitely request".

Building Web Applications with ArcGIS was designed for web developers who don't necessarily have an experience of ArcGIS. There are going to be three themes running throughout the book. The first theme is design, which is covered in the first two chapters of this book. We will discuss how to interpret requirements, create the interface design, and add basic functionalities such as loading the map. The second theme is development, which is covered in *Chapter 3, Querying ArcGIS Services*. This is where the reader will add more functionalities such as querying and interacting with the map. The last theme is enrichment and is covered in *Chapter 4, Rich Content and Mobile Integration* and *Chapter 5, Posting Reviews, Ratings, and Photos*. It is designed for advanced readers. It will show how to do editing, querying related information, and mobile integration.

All the three themes come under the umbrella of a project called "Bestaurants", where the reader helps a client in Belize, a country on the northeastern coast of Central America. The reader will help improve the Bestaurants project by designing a web interface to visualize the best restaurants, diners, café, and so on in Belize. With each chapter, the Bestaurants' client will ask for new requirements, which the reader will try to implement by the end of the chapter.

What this book covers

Chapter 1, The Bestaurants Project, contains a full description of the Bestaurants project. It breaks down the requirements into small pieces that will be executed in the next four chapters. This chapter will also include some introduction about map services, JavaScript API, and how to set up the necessary web services.

Chapter 2, Setting Up the Basic Web Application, teaches you how to get started with a basic map web page based on the design proposed in *Chapter 1, The Bestaurants Project*. You will set up the web server, create a simple HTML page, and add necessary code to show the map service published in the previous chapter. You will be able to gradually, throughout the next chapters, fill the page with functionalities.

Chapter 3, Querying ArcGIS Services, teaches you to communicate with the services to query, retrieve, and display the results now that you have developed a basic web viewer website.

Chapter 4, Rich Content and Mobile Integration, makes the web application more interactive by adding more rich tools. You will query and display the related records and do some calculations with the results. This chapter will also enable our site to be viewed on mobile.

Chapter 5, *Posting Reviews, Ratings, and Photos*, introduces the feature service and editing. It will show you how your client can post restaurant reviews, ratings, and photos.

Appendix, *Bestaurants on ArcGIS Online*, discusses an alternative way to implement the web applications using ArcGIS online.

What you need for this book

For this book, you'll require:

- A Windows machine running Windows Server 2008 R2 SP1, preferably, since this is what the book is using Windows 7 and 8 will also work..

- Esri ArcGIS for Desktop 10.2.x or 10.1 to publish the map service. The book uses ArcGIS 10.2. You can download a trial version from `http://www.esri.com/products/free-trials` or order from your local Esri distributor.

- Esri ArcGIS for Server 10.2.x or 10.1 to host the map service. This book uses ArcGIS for Server 10.2. You can order a trial version from your local Esri distributor.

Who this book is for

The book is tailored for web developers who want to learn how to use their skills to write web mapping applications for ArcGIS. The reader doesn't require any ArcGIS knowledge.

Conventions

In this book, you will find a number of text styles that distinguish between different kinds of information. Here are some examples of these styles and an explanation of their meaning.

Code words in text, database table names, folder names, filenames, file extensions, pathnames, dummy URLs, user input, and Twitter handles are shown as follows: "We will install all the software on a single machine called `ARCGISMACHINE`."

A block of code is set as follows:

```
<html>
<body>
<h1>Hello, ArcGIS! </h1>
</body>
</html>
```

When we wish to draw your attention to a particular part of a code block, the relevant lines or items are set in bold:

```
dojo.require("esri.map");
dojo.require("esri.dijit.Legend");
function startup()
```

New terms and **important words** are shown in bold. Words that you see on the screen, for example, in menus or dialog boxes, appear in the text like this: "Click on **ArcGIS JavaScript** to view the map service."

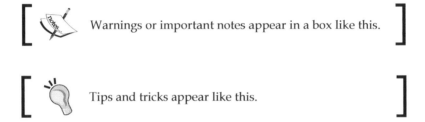

> Warnings or important notes appear in a box like this.

> Tips and tricks appear like this.

Reader feedback

Feedback from our readers is always welcome. Let us know what you think about this book—what you liked or disliked. Reader feedback is important for us as it helps us develop titles that you will really get the most out of.

To send us general feedback, simply e-mail feedback@packtpub.com, and mention the book's title in the subject of your message.

If there is a topic that you have expertise in and you are interested in either writing or contributing to a book, see our author guide at www.packtpub.com/authors.

Customer support

Now that you are the proud owner of a Packt book, we have a number of things to help you to get the most from your purchase.

Downloading the example code

You can download the example code files from your account at `http://www.packtpub.com` for all the Packt Publishing books you have purchased. If you purchased this book elsewhere, you can visit `http://www.packtpub.com/support` and register to have the files e-mailed directly to you.

Errata

Although we have taken every care to ensure the accuracy of our content, mistakes do happen. If you find a mistake in one of our books—maybe a mistake in the text or the code—we would be grateful if you could report this to us. By doing so, you can save other readers from frustration and help us improve subsequent versions of this book. If you find any errata, please report them by visiting `http://www.packtpub.com/submit-errata`, selecting your book, clicking on the **Errata Submission Form** link, and entering the details of your errata. Once your errata are verified, your submission will be accepted and the errata will be uploaded to our website or added to any list of existing errata under the Errata section of that title.

To view the previously submitted errata, go to `https://www.packtpub.com/books/content/support` and enter the name of the book in the search field. The required information will appear under the **Errata** section.

Piracy

Piracy of copyrighted material on the Internet is an ongoing problem across all media. At Packt, we take the protection of our copyright and licenses very seriously. If you come across any illegal copies of our works in any form on the Internet, please provide us with the location address or website name immediately so that we can pursue a remedy.

Please contact us at `copyright@packtpub.com` with a link to the suspected pirated material.

We appreciate your help in protecting our authors and our ability to bring you valuable content.

Questions

If you have a problem with any aspect of this book, you can contact us at `questions@packtpub.com`, and we will do our best to address the problem.

1

The Bestaurants Project

The Web has proved to be the most resilient technology ever since its invention. New technologies have risen and died down against the rapid pace of technology advancement and the user adaptation. However, the Web remains the most used technology due to its open standard and accessibility. The idea of having a thin browser that can consume content over a network from a remote server seems to be the most intelligent and intuitive design ever created. The client is completely isolated from the gimmicks of the server: what version, references, dependencies of the software, operating system, and so on. All the browser has to support is HTTP. Not only that, the web applications can also reflect on business budget, as it eliminates expensive hardware budget, software licenses, and it can even extend the number of users.

 Hypertext Transfer Protocol (HTTP) is a standard protocol for transferring structured text information between client and server.

Seeing its formidability, companies looking to reach a wider client base with the least cost started adopting the Web into their enterprises. Desktop applications started moving to the Web. I can still remember the days when I used to search for applications to convert an image to an icon file so that I can use it in my projects. I had to make sure that I had the right operating system to install the software and install any dependencies if needed. Now, with the *ICO converter* website www.icoconverter.com, I simply upload my image, and the website returns the icon file. Similarly, to create a ringtone for my phone, I can edit and cut my favorite part of the mp3 music file by uploading it to www.mp3cut.net, then specifying where to cut, and then download the new mp3 file.

Among the companies that started to adopt the Web is Esri, the top geographic information system software provider with its *ArcGIS flagship software*. Esri's main successful software is **ArcGIS for Desktop**, hereafter known as Desktop (uppercase). This rich software was built for Microsoft Windows and it has had a lot of success. However, to view the geographic data created by ArcGIS for Desktop, one should have this software installed on his or her PC. This takes resources, time, and more licenses, making users frown upon using it, especially those who don't use Windows as their primary operating system. Also, companies adopting the ArcGIS technology have to pay extra for licensing for each user on the desktop.

- **ArcGIS**: This is the proprietary technology, from Esri, that helps author, edit, publish, and view geographic content.

- **ArcGIS for Desktop**: This is a 32-bit desktop application running on Microsoft Windows that allows for creating, editing, viewing, and analyzing of geographic content.

That is why Esri designed a new solution which enables users to consume geographic and mapping data from a browser. This software is called ArcGIS for Server. It allows the user to publish geographic content as a *web service* that can be used from different terminals. It also enables mobile devices to consume GIS data, something that traditionally was limited to desktop application only. The *Online Audio Cutter* website, for instance, has a web service that is being called from the main page to execute the file cutting process and returns the new modified file.

ArcGIS for Server is an integrated solution, which is becoming the backbone for the ArcGIS technology. The solution is scalable, meaning that you can add more machines to increase the performance. The installation of ArcGIS for Server is outside the scope of this book. You can learn how to install, configure, tune, and administer ArcGIS for Server from my other book, *Administering ArcGIS for Server*, published by *Packt Publishing*.

ArcGIS for Server: This is a solution that allows users to publish geographic content as a web service and use it from any client that supports HTTP. You can read more about ArcGIS for Server here:

```
http://webhelp.esri.com/arcgisserver/9.2/dotnet/
manager/concepts/whats_server.htm
```

Web service: This is a method that can be called by a client to perform a particular task and return some results.

In this book, you will work on a fictional business project named Bestaurants, where you will learn how to design and develop a completely functional ArcGIS web application that allows you to view Bestaurants's database of restaurants. This chapter will focus on setting up the basics and the fundamentals that will help you get started. We will read and understand the project mission requirements, design an interface and architecture, set up the Web server, and develop the template for our web application.

Getting started with Bestaurants

To start working with this chapter, there are some prerequisites that need to be in place. Make sure you have a Windows machine with a minimum of 6 GB of RAM with the following software installed on it:

- Microsoft .NET Framework 3.5 SP1: If you are using Windows 7 or higher, this framework can be found and downloaded from `http://www.microsoft.com/en-us/download/details.aspx?id=25150`. If you are using Windows Server, it can be installed from the application roles.

- ArcGIS for Desktop 10.1 media or higher: You can download the latest version of ArcGIS for Desktop for free with a 60-day trial period from the Esri website: `http://www.esri.com/software/arcgis/arcgis-for-desktop/free-trial`. At the time of writing, Esri was on Version 10.2.2. You will need at least a standard or an advanced license, which will allow you to view and publish services.

- ArcGIS for Server 10.1 media installer or higher: This will host the service that we will publish and that we will eventually use to write our application. You can request a trial from your local Esri distributor, and take a look at my other book *Administering ArcGIS for Server*, published by *Packt Publishing*, to install it. This can be hosted on the same machine.

I will be using Windows Server 2008 R2 SP1 as the operating system, ArcGIS for Desktop 10.2, and ArcGIS for Server 10.2. We will install all the software on a single machine called ARCGISMACHINE.

 If you already have ArcGIS for Server installed in another location, that is fine; just make sure to update your code to the correct server accordingly whenever we mention ArcGIS for Server.

In *Appendix, Bestaurants on ArcGIS Online*, we will learn how to replace ArcGIS for Server with ArcGIS Online as our GIS data store.

Bestaurants, the best restaurants in Belize

It has been proven that it's easy to learn a new concept by actually implementing that concept in a real-life project scenario. That is why we created this fictional project. Reading the project statement and requirements will teleport you in to the context of a developer who has to analyze, design, and implement instead of just being a reader. This helps you guess how you will be able to do things instead of being spoon-fed and bombarded by information. We will start small, from concepts you will probably be familiar with, which will give you the confidence to progress through the book. We will slowly develop and plug in the components into the main website until the whole website is completed. At the end of each chapter, I will provide a support file with the last chapter on the website, just in case you decided to skip through a chapter, you can pick up things from the previous chapter.

 This project is an example that will be used and it will keep on reappearing in the following chapters. This is not an actual project and not related to the country whatsoever.

The project statement

Belize is thriving in tourism. Lots of tourists go there on holidays to enjoy its beautiful beaches and a wide range of restaurants. The government of Belize is trying to enrich tourists' experience in finding their favorite restaurants in the country more effectively. To accomplish that, a new project titled **Bestaurants** has been proposed to design a website to feature the best restaurants in Belize. For that, they asked for the website to be able to run on both desktop browsers and mobile devices.

The website will contain a map that shows the city of Belize and the restaurants with key icons based on the restaurant type. For example, a café will be shown as a coffee mug and a restaurant will be displayed as a fork and knife. Tourists should be able to search for restaurants by name, category, or rating. The results should show the ratings, reviews, and pictures of that restaurant if available. The user will only be able to upload photos and write reviews. When the user opens the website from his mobile phone or a tablet, they should get the exact same functionalities that are available in the web version. Finally, the website will identify and show the user location on the map using the **Global Positioning System (GPS)** receiver on the device. The user can then highlight all restaurants near them by clicking on a button.

GPS: Global Positioning System provides the location and time information using satellites on the earth. Nearly all new smart phones are equipped with GPS receivers that can identify the device location with respect to Earth. You can read more about GPS here:

```
http://www.gps.gov/
```

Proposed Interface Design

Before we start the development, we need to get a picture of what the website would look like after it is completed. That is what is called the **Interface Design**; we can do it on a piece of paper or using sophisticated software such as Microsoft Visio. What is important is to capture what the website should look like.

Interface Design: This is the heart of any web application, which defines how the website will look like and function. The general rule of thumb is to keep the interface simple.

Let's start designing our canvas; we will start with the most important element of the website: the map. I know that there will be a map because the project statement says:

The website will contain a map that shows the city of Belize and the restaurants with key icons based on the restaurant type.

The map will display the restaurants, and the user will be interacting with it. The map should be the biggest object on the site as it will be the focus point for the user. The map will need zoom functionality, so we will add a small slider to the top to help the user zoom in or zoom out. Moreover, the user will require a legend to show the key objects on the map; so we will reserve a space for that as well. Reserving 25 percent of the left side of the website will suffice for the legend. The following figure illustrates what the application page design will look like. Remember that the design can be changed as we progress through the chapters.

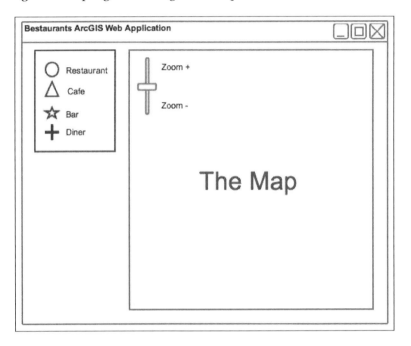

The website looks simple and *zen*, but unfortunately, we cannot keep it this simple. We need to add more elements to the design. Read the following quote from the project statement:

> *Tourists should be able to search for restaurants by name, category, or rating. The results should show the rating of the restaurant, reviews, and pictures of that restaurant if available.*

This quote implies that we should have a search box and probably a drop-down list for the category and rating. The bottom line is that there will be some input controls that the user will interact with; so we need to reserve a space for it. Let's reserve the upper 10 percent of the web page for input controls. We also need some space to display the search result where we can display the restaurant name, rating, reviews, and photos. For this, we can use the left area, below the legend. The new Interface Design is illustrated in the following figure:

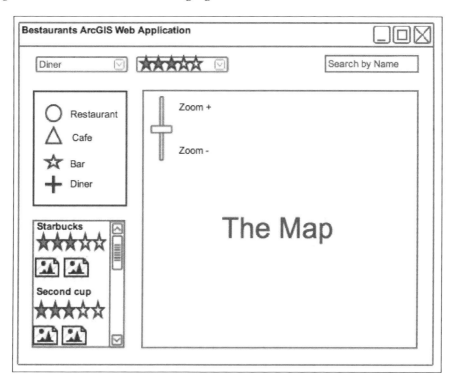

As the user searches and interacts with the map, it will be nice to display some status and loading messages for them. Let's save the bottom five percent of the page for status messages.

Of course, this design is not written on stone, so you might want to move things around as you progress through the book. Take a look at our initial Interface Design:

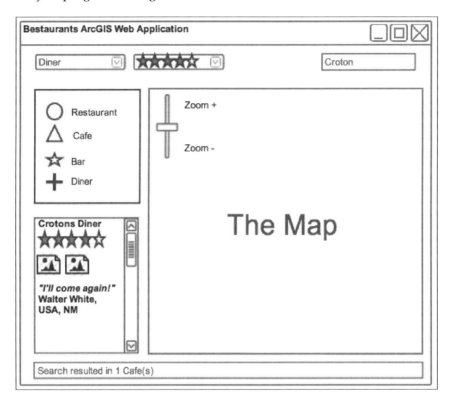

The proposed architecture

Before rushing in to the developing process, it is always good practice to create the architecture of your components. This helps show how the entire solution is tied together. The architecture describes the software, hardware components, the relations between them and assess in viewing the solution as a whole. With the architecture, the developer can see the big picture before diving into the details of implementation, which may save them a lot of time and make them consider exterior elements. You can read more about system architecture at:

http://www.esri.com/library/whitepapers/pdfs/sysdesig.pdf

The first part of the architecture is to make a decision on what programming language is suitable for the web application. This can only be determined by reading the requirements. Let's take a look at the following quote from the project statement:

The Client asked for the site to run on both desktop browsers and mobile devices.

The best option to make a web application able to run on both mobile and desktop is to use a language that will run on both. ArcGIS provides *APIs* for *Silverlight*, *Flex*, and *JavaScript*. Silverlight and Flex are good and simple programming languages and provide rich interface and logic; however, they both require browser plugins to run, and no smart phone supports it, so they are out of the question. This leaves us with the *ArcGIS JavaScript API* to develop our web application. The reason we chose JavaScript is that this scripting language is open standard and can run in modern browsers including mobile devices. JavaScript is a client-side scripting language, which means all the code executes on the client. Keep that in mind while we design the architecture. Note that JavaScript API is a volatile SDK and a continually evolving API. Esri continually releases updates for this library at least twice a year, adding new functionally in each update. It is crucial to mind which version you are developing on, use one, stick to it, and upgrade as you see new functionalities that you would like to use. Fortunately, this API can work with services shared and published on ArcGIS Online, which makes it a really good choice.

API: Application Programming Interface is a set of functionalities that are exposed for the developers to extend and customize particular software; in our case, this software is ArcGIS.

Silverlight: Silverlight was created by Microsoft. This is a rich structured language that runs on the client, but requires a special plugin to be translated in the browser.

Flex: Flex was created by Adobe. This is a rich programming language that provides rich content on the web and requires a special plugin to run on a browser.

ArcGIS JavaScript API: This is an application programming interface exposed as a JavaScript library that is used with ArcGIS for Server services. This API can run on modern browsers and mobile devices without a plugin.

Now that we have selected our programming language, there are four main components we can look at in our Bestaurants project. The components are listed as follows:

- The database that contains the restaurant's data.

- The ArcGIS for Server site that connects to the database.

- The web server where our web application will be hosted and where the clients will connect to browse the website.

- The client browser, which will connect to the web server to retrieve the website. Take a look at the following figure for more details:

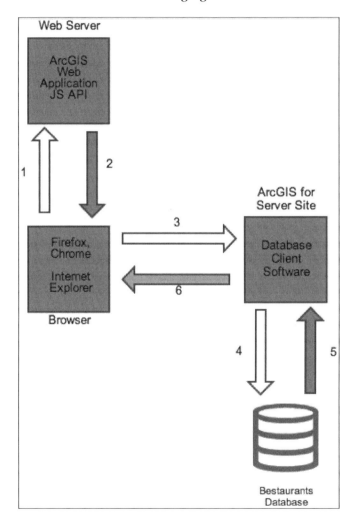

Let's explain this design, from the moment a user opens the web application up until the moment they are served the map, in the following steps:

1. The user opens the browser and types the address of the web server hosting the web application that we will be writing. This will send an HTTP request to the web server.

2. The web server receives the user HTTP request and returns the content of the website back to the user.

3. Since the scripting language is JavaScript, the browser starts executing the code locally on the browser side. The ArcGIS JavaScript code that you will write in *Chapter 2*, *Setting Up the Basic Web Application*, will create an HTTP request to the ArcGIS for Server site for the Bestaurants web service.

4. ArcGIS for Server site receives the HTTP request from the client, and converts the HTTP request into a **Structured Query Language (SQL)** query to be sent to the database.

5. The database executes the query and returns the result to ArcGIS for Server.

6. ArcGIS for Server wraps the results into an HTTP request and returns it back to the client.

 SQL: Structured query language, is a language designed to retrieve data from a database. The syntax of this language depends on the type of the database.

In our case, the web server, ArcGIS for Server and the database components are located on a single machine named ARCGISMACHINE. You can choose to put each component in a separate server, which is a good practice for scaling each component independently later.

Installing ArcGIS software

In this section, we will quickly install and configure both ArcGIS for Desktop and ArcGIS for Server on your new machine so that we can carry on with the exercise. You will need the ArcGIS for Desktop and ArcGIS for Server media CD-ROM. We will start by installing ArcGIS for Desktop, which uses the default installation configurations, and then we will install and configure ArcGIS for Server.

Installing ArcGIS for Desktop

Before we start, we need to install Microsoft .NET Framework 3.5 SP1, which can be found in the installation media. Follow these steps to start the installation:

1. Log in to the machine as the administrator user or any user who has administrative privileges on this machine. I will be using the `Administrator` user.

2. Install Microsoft .NET Framework 3.5 SP1 and wait for the installation to finish. If you are using Windows Server, the framework can be installed from **Server Manager** by adding the **Application Server** role (see the following screenshot for more details). If the application server role is already installed, it will be marked as **(Installed)**, as shown in the following screenshot:

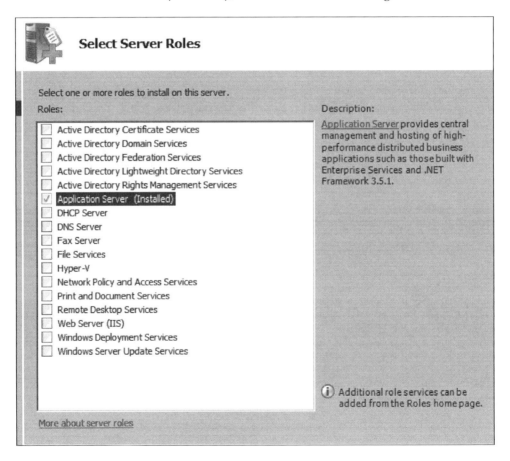

3. After you install the framework, go ahead and run the ArcGIS for Desktop installation file. Make sure you don't have any previous ArcGIS installations on this machine. You can read the following online guide to install ArcGIS for Desktop:

   `http://resources.esri.com/help/9.3/arcgisdesktop/installGuides/ArcGIS_Desktop/whnjs.htm`

4. After the installation is complete, authorize the product by providing it with the proper license. You can get a 60-day trial version from the product website (`www.esri.com`).

5. ArcGIS for Desktop installs two main applications, ArcMap and ArcCatalog both of which we will be using in this book. ArcMap will be the software, which views and authors the map, and ArcCatalog will be used to manage the GIS database.

6. Close the installation dialog and restart your machine.

Installing ArcGIS for Server

Now we need to install and configure ArcGIS for Server. We need to work with Version 10.1 and above since prior to that, ArcGIS for Server had a different architecture. Follow these steps to install ArcGIS for Server:

1. Log in to the machine as the administrator user or any user who has administrative privilege on this machine. I will be using the `Administrator` user.

2. Run the installation file for ArcGIS for Server and choose ArcGIS for Server.

3. Accept and approve the license agreement and click on **Next**.

4. In the **Select Features** dialog box, make sure all features are selected to be installed and click on **Next**.

5. Keep the default path for Python and click on **Next**.

6. In the Specify ArcGIS Server account, type in the Windows username and password you have used. Remember, it should have administrator privileges. In my case, it is the **Administrator** user. Click on **Next** to continue, as shown in the following screenshot:

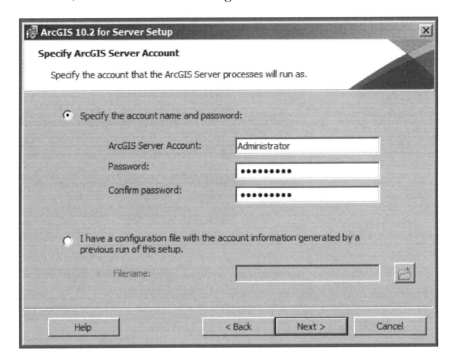

7. Choose to not export the configuration file and click on **Next**.

8. Click on **Install** to start the installation process.

9. When the installation is complete, the installer will ask you to authorize your ArcGIS for Server. Use the license provided by your Esri distributor and click on **Finish**.

10. A browser with a new website will be opened. This will ask you to create a new server site or join an existing one. Choose to **Create New Site** and click on **Next**.

 If you accidently closed this browser, you can get to it by typing http://ARCGISMACHINE:6080/arcgis/ manager, where ARCGISMACHINE is the machine you installed ArcGIS for Server on. The following link will work as well: http://localhost:6080/arcgis/manager.

11. In the **Primary Site Administrator account** page, type siteadmin in the **Username** section, enter a password, and click on **Next**. This is the account we will use to publish the Bestaurant service to ArcGIS for Server. Make sure to remember these credentials.

12. Keep the default configuration directories and click on **Next**.

13. In the **Configuration Summary**, click on **Finish**. You should see a similar summary page as shown in the following screenshot:

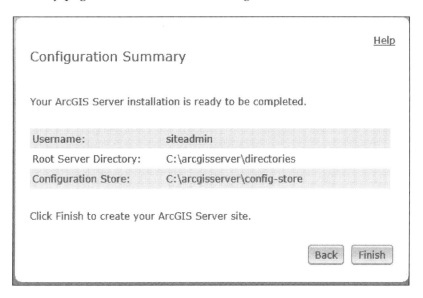

14. Close the browser and restart your machine.

You just finished installing ArcGIS for Desktop and Server. Next we will look at to publishing the service.

 Note that this is a very basic installation manual and should not be followed for production environment. For advanced configurations and production setup, read my other book *Administering ArcGIS for Server*, published by Packt Publishing. You can also read more about this in the Esri online documentation (http://resources.esri.com/).

Publishing a service in ArcGIS for Server

We have our interface and architecture, now we need to publish our Bestaurants database in ArcGIS for Server. We just completed setting up ArcGIS for Server and Desktop. You must have ArcGIS for Desktop and ArcGIS for Server installed, configured, and ready for use to be able to perform this exercise.

Downloading the example code

You can download the example code files for all Packt books you have purchased from your account at http://www.packtpub.com. If you purchased this book elsewhere, you can visit http://www.packtpub.com/ and register to have the files e-mailed directly to you.

We need to get the supporting files for this chapter: 29550T_01_Files. This file can be downloaded from www.packtpub.com. Copy this folder to the ARCGISMACHINE machine. Follow these steps to publish the service on ArcGIS for Server.

1. Log in to the machine with the administrator account.

2. Go to the root C: drive and create a new folder named 29550T. Copy the folder named 29550T_01_Files from the code bundle to the 29550T folder.

3. Open the 29550T_01_Files folder and double-click on the MXD file Belize.mxd. This will open ArcMap, which will allow us to view the Bestaurants restaurants data on ArcGIS for Desktop.

The MXD file or the map document file is what you get when you save a map in ArcMap. It contains basic configuration, extent, symbologies, and legends.

4. When ArcMap opens, you should see the data as shown in the following screenshot:

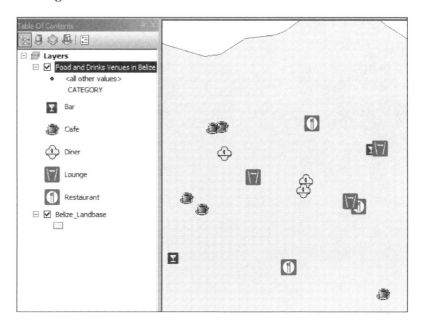

5. From the **File** menu, point to **Share As** and then click on **Service ....**

6. Select **Publish a Service** and click on **Next**.

7. From the **Choose a connection** drop-down list, click on **Create New Connection** icon as shown in the following screenshot:

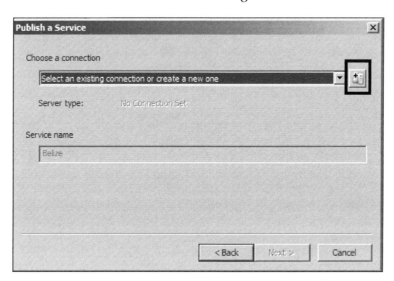

8. From the **Add ArcGIS Server** dialog box, select **Publish GIS Services** and click on **Next**.

9. In the **General** dialog box, enter `http://ARCGISMACHINE:6080/arcgis` in the **Server URL** textbox. Remember, `ARCGISMACHINE` is where you have installed ArcGIS for Server. In the **Server Type** textbox, select **ArcGIS Server** and type in your `siteadmin` credentials in the authentication box and click on **Finish**. This is all shown in the following screenshot:

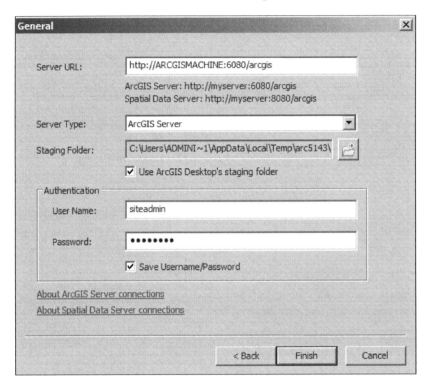

10. In the **Publish a Service** dialog box, enter `Bestaurants` as the **Service Name** and click on **Next**.

11. Keep the option **Use existing folder** enabled and click on **Continue** to start the Service Editor.

12. In the Service Editor, click on **Publish**.

13. If you were prompted with the **Copying data to Server** message, simply click **OK**. This will copy the **Bestaurants** data to a cached location. You can read more about caching at `http://webhelp.esri.com/arcgisserver/9.3/dotNet/what_is_map_caching.htm`.

14. After a while, you should get the following message prompting that the service has been published:

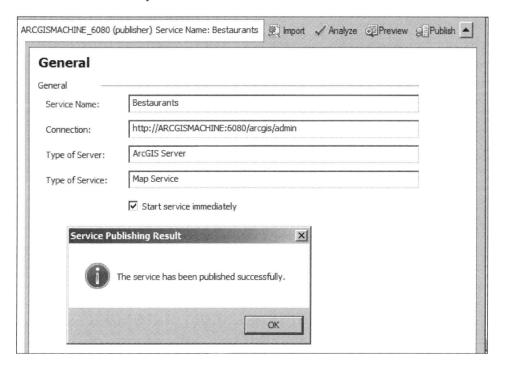

Testing the published service

Now that we have published our Bestaurants service, it is time for us to test whether it is working. Luckily, ArcGIS provides a nice way for testing our services; however, you will be requiring an Internet connection to test them. Go ahead and follow these steps for testing our services:

1. Open your browser and type in the following address:
   `http://ARCGISMACHINE:6080/arcgis/rest`.

2. Click on **Bestaurants (MapServer)**.

3. Click on **ArcGIS JavaScript** to view the map service.

You should see the restaurants of Belize on the web now, which means that your service works perfectly and it is ready to be used for our web application. Take a look at the following screenshot that shows the Bestaurants service data:

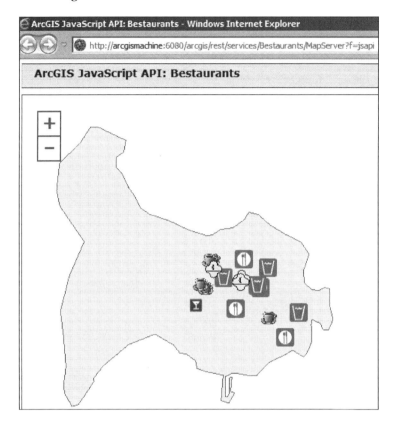

Congratulations! You just completed your first basic GIS web application. But we still have a long run to tackle all the client's requirements.

Summary

In this chapter, you were introduced to Bestaurants, a web application project for the tourists in Belize to view and search for Belize's best restaurants. We designed the interface of the Bestaurants web application and created a software architecture that will help us in the development process. We learned how a request is executed from the point it is initiated on the browser up until it gets executed in the database and returned. We have installed and configured both ArcGIS for Desktop and ArcGIS for Server from scratch. Finally, we have published the Bestaurants data to ArcGIS for Server as a service and tested that it is working.

In the next chapter, we will build the web application template in HTML and use basic ArcGIS JavaScript API command to connect to the service we published.

2
Setting Up the Basic Web Application

In the previous chapter, we introduced the Bestaurants project. We proposed an interface that gave us a good idea of what the web application will look like based on the project requirements. We also designed an architecture, which illustrated the different components that the project will consist of. We haven't done any development but we managed to set up ArcGIS for Desktop and ArcGIS for Server, and published the Bestaurants database as a service.

In this chapter, we will set up the web server on which the web application will run. We will spend the rest of the chapter implementing the interface we designed in the previous chapter and will add some ArcGIS code that will connect to the service we have published. We will slowly continue adding functionalities to the web application. This theme will continue throughout the book until the web application is completed in the last chapter.

For this chapter, it is recommended that you install both *Notepad*++ and *Google Chrome*. Notepad ++ is a great text editor that you can download for free from `http://notepad-plus-plus.org/`. It will help us throughout the rest of the chapters, and Chrome has great built-in debugging tools for developers to troubleshoot code, monitor browser requests and more. This is something Internet Explorer lacks as of the latest version IE 11. Google Chrome can be downloaded from `http://www.google.com/chrome`.

Setting up the web server

If you have developed websites before, you know that you need to host your site on a web server such as *Apache* and **Internet Information Server (IIS)**. I will be using IIS, specifically Version 7, in the course of this book; however, feel free to use any other web server you prefer.

> **Apache** is an open source web server which can support multiple operating systems.
>
> **IIS** stands for Internet Information Server which is the proprietary web server for Microsoft Windows.

Installing IIS

Installing IIS is easy; however, the installation procedure differs based on the operating system you are using. The following steps show how to install it on Windows Server:

1. Open **Server Manager**, you can find it on the taskbar by default or you can type `ServerManager.msc` in the run dialog box to access it.

2. From the **Server Manager** tree on the left-hand side, right-click on the **Roles** node then click on **Add Roles** as shown in the following screenshot:

3. Click on **Next** on the **Before you Begin** page.

4. In the **Select Server Roles** window, select **Web Server (IIS)** and click on **Next** as illustrated in the following screenshot:

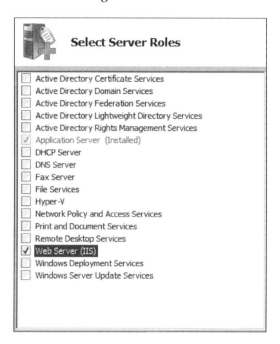

5. In the **Select Server Roles** window, select **Web Server (IIS)** and click on **Next** as illustrated in the preceding screenshot.

6. Click on **Next** in the **Web Server (IIS)** page.

7. In the **Select Role Service** window, we need the **Active Server Pages (ASP)** component from the IIS. Under **Application Development**, select **ASP** and you will be prompted to install the required role services, select **Agree**, and then click on **Next**. Refer to the following screenshot for more details:

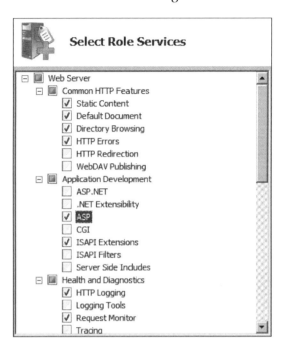

ASP is a basic server side language that doesn't need a special development environment like Visual Studio to be installed. That is why I like using it for testing and showing cases. All you need is a notepad and you can write your own website. However, for complex applications, it is better to use ASP.NET.

8. Click on **Install** to complete the installation of IIS.

9. Click on **Close** after the installation has finished.

You just installed the web server. Now you are ready to start writing the web applications.

 If you are using Windows 7 or Windows 8, you can perform this procedure using the **user interface (UI)** or a script. In **Control Panel**, click on **Programs** and then click on **Turn Windows features on or off**. In the **Windows Features** dialog box, click on **Internet Information Services** and then click on **OK**. To do it yourself, you can follow the tutorial at http://qr.net/iiswin.

Testing the web server

To test our web server, we need to write a simple HTML code and run it on the server using the following steps:

1. Open Notepad++ and write the following code in it:

```html
<html>
<body>
<h1>Hello, ArcGIS! </h1>
</body>
</html>
```

2. Save the file into the location: `c:\inetpub\wwwroot` and name the file as `helloarcgis.html`. This folder will not be available before you install the IIS web server. Take a look at the following screenshot for illustrations:

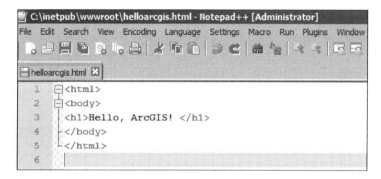

3. Open Chrome and type the following in the address bar: `http://arcgismachine/helloarcgis.html` and press *Enter*. You should see the following page, which means that your web server is working fine:

You can also use the IP address instead of the machine name to access the web server. My server IP is `192.168.1.7`, so to access it the URL will be: `http://192.168.1.7/helloarcgis.html`.

Setting up the ArcGIS web application

As you may know, any web application can be accessed through an *address* and a *port*. This is how you uniquely define a website. For example, `www.packtpub.com`, which can also be written as `www.packtpub.com:80`, this means the website is hosting on the default HTTP port `80`. Port 80 is the default HTTP port and that is why browsers ignore it.

> The **Address** consists of the IP address, hostname, or domain name of the web server where the web application is running. The examples are `192.168.1.2`, `ARCGISMACHINE` or `www.packtpub.com`. You can get the IP address by using the `IPConfig` command in the command prompt.
>
> The **Port** is an integer number assigned to a server that acts as a door to which a client can connect through. Ports can be secured and blocked with the help of a firewall to prevent malicious access by unauthorized users.

In this section, we will first write the HTML web page; for this you will need to know some basic HTML code. Then we will inject the HTML with what we were waiting for, a map. A map is no fun without data to show, so we will add some ArcGIS JavaScript code to load the Bestaurants service into the map.

Creating the HTML web page

For this exercise, we will need to refer to the interface we designed in *Chapter 1*, *The Bestaurants Project*. The following screenshot shows that interface:

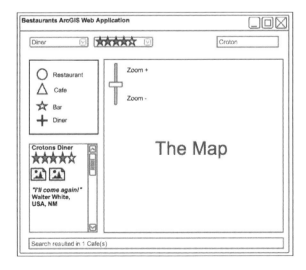

We can easily break down this page into a single layout table, having four rows with two columns. The first row will contain the toolbar and will stretch through the entire table that occupies 10 percent of the page height. The second and the third rows contain the legend and the search results which both occupy 20 percent of the page width and around 40 percent of its height. The second column of the second and third rows stretches the map with 80 percent remaining width and 85 percent height of the page. What remains is the lower status bar, which stretches the entire page width and only occupies 5 percent of page. If you sum the element's heights and widths, you will get both 100 percent. Take a look at the following breakdown figure of our interface:

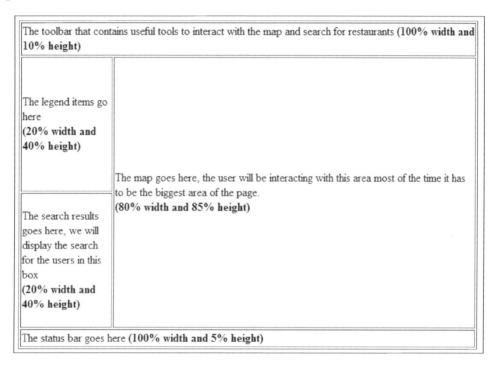

The following is the HTML code equivalent of the preceding breakdown figure. The HTML code can be found in the supporting files for this chapter: 2955OT_02_Files\ Code named bestaurants01_structure.html.

```
<html>
  <head>
    <title>Bestaurants Web Application</title>
  </head>
  <body>
```

```
<table border =1 width = '1000px' height = '700px'
  align =center>
  <tr>
    <td colspan =2 width='100%' height ='10%'>

      <!-- The toolbar where we will place tools -->
      The toolbar that contains useful tools to interact with the
map and search for restaurants  <b> (100% width and 10% height) </b>
    </td>
  </tr>
  <tr>
    <td width='20%' height ='40%'>
      <!-- The legend of the map goes here -->
      The legend items go here <br> <b>(20% width and 40% height)
</b>
    </td>
    <td width='80%' height ='85%' rowspan =2>
      <!-- The ArcGIS Map will be displayed here -->
      The map goes here, the user will be interacting with this
area most of the time it has to be the biggest area of the page.<br>
      <b>(80% width and 85% height)</b>
    </td>
  </tr>
  <tr>
    <td width='20%' height ='40%'>
      <!-- The search results will go here -->
      The search results goes here, we will display the search for
the users in this box <br> <b>(20% width and 40% height)</b>
    </td>
  </tr>
  <tr>
    <td colspan =2 width='100%' height ='5%'>
      <!-- The status bar for displaying messages goes here
        -->
      The status bar goes here  <b> (100% width and 5% height)</b>
    </td>
  </tr>
</table>
</body>
</html>
```

Copy the file to the `c:\inetpub\wwwroot` location and rename it to `mybestaurants.html`. Run the web application by launching the URL `http://arcgismachine/mybestaurants.html`. This will be the file you will be modifying from now on. I will still be providing you with the end results HTML file after each change; however, it will be better if you could modify the file yourself before looking at the end result.

Adding the map and loading the ArcGIS service

Now that we have the skeleton of our web application, it is time to write some ArcGIS code. Up until now, we only used basic HTML; in this section, we will use ArcGIS JavaScript API to add the map. The JavaScript API uses *dojo toolkit* for its development.

Dojo toolkit is a rich set of JavaScript library tools that simplifies development in JavaScript. You can learn more about ArcGIS JavaScript API from the Esri developer website at `https://developers.arcgis.com/javascript/`

We need to reference the API in `mybestaurants.html` that you have copied to the `inetpub` folder. Follow these steps to add the map to your `mybestaurants.html` file:

1. In the supporting files `2955OT_02_Files\Library`, copy the `arcgisjs` folder to `c:\inetpub\wwwroot`. This contains the ArcGIS JavaScript library Version 3.10 which I made ready for you to use.

2. Edit `mybestaurants.html` with Notepad ++ and add the following style reference to the header element. This will inherit the necessary styling attributes for our map and layout:

```
<html>
  <head>
    <title>Bestaurants Web Application</title>
    <link rel="stylesheet" href="arcgisjs/esri.css">
...
```

3. Add the following script reference to the header element. This is the path to the `init.js` file which contains the necessary code to run the ArcGIS JavaScript API:

```
...
<head>
  <title>Bestaurants Web Application</title>
    <link rel="stylesheet" href="arcgisjs/esri.css">
    <script src="arcgisjs/3.10/init.js"></script>
</head>
...
```

4. Next, we need to add a function that will be initiated when the web application runs; we will use it to load the map and to run other initialization code. This is called the `startup` function and it will be the pillar of our development. Add the script in the header element as illustrated in the next code snippet. After that we need to add the code, `dojo.addOnLoad(startup)`, which will tell the browser to call the `startup` function upon starting. The `startup` function currently contains an alert message just to test if the things are working:

```
...
<head>
  <title>Bestaurants Web Application</title>
  <link rel="stylesheet" href="arcgisjs/esri.css">
  <script src="arcgisjs/3.10/init.js"></script>
  <script>
    function startup()
    {
      alert("map is about to load");
    }
  dojo.addOnLoad(startup);
  </script>
</head>
...
```

5. Save the `mybestaurants.html` file and run it. You should get the following message when you try the URL `http://arcgismachine/mybestaurants.html`:

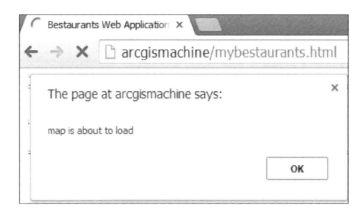

6. Now we need to add a few more lines. The div element will contain the map, the reference to `Esri.map`, and some code to create a map object. Find `<!-- The ArcGIS Map will be displayed here -->` and replace it along with the text given in the following code with a div element highlighted. The `class = 'arcgismap'` term will inherit some style attributes from `esri.css` which will properly show and scale the map to fit in our table:

```
...
<tr>
  <td width='20%' height ='40%'>
    <!-- The legend of the map goes here -->
    The legend items go here <br> <b>(20% width and 40% height) </
b>
  </td>
  <td width='80%' height ='85%' rowspan =2>
    <div id = 'mymap' class = 'arcgismap' >

    </div>
  </td>
</tr>
...
```

7. Next, add `dojo.require("esri.map")` in the second script element just before the `startup` function. This will reference the necessary map-related references to the application:

```
...
<script src="arcgisjs/3.10/init.js"></script>
<script>
  dojo.require("esri.map");
  function startup()
  {
    alert("map is about to load");
  }
  dojo.addOnLoad(startup);
</script>
...
```

8. In the `startup` function, we will create the map object and then use it to add our Bestaurants service. The `esri.Map("mymap")` term will create a map object, which we got by referencing `esri.map`, and add it to the `mymap` div element. The `ArcGISDynamicMapServiceLayer` class is a class which is also imported from `esri.map` and which will create a layer from the service we published in the previous chapter. Each service has a unique URL that points to it and allows for clients to utilize it. The structure is: `http://arcgisservermachine:6080/arcgis/rest/services/SERVICE_NAME/MapServer`. Finally, `map.addLayer` will add the layer to the map:

```
function startup()
{
  alert("map is about to load");
  //create the map object and load it in 'mymap' div element
  var map = new esri.Map("mymap");
  //load the layer into an object
  var lyr = new esri.layers.ArcGISDynamicMapServiceLayer
  ( "http://arcgismachine:6080/arcgis/rest/services/
    Bestaurants/MapServer"
  );

//add the layer to map
  map.addLayer(lyr);}
}
```

 The service endpoint provides useful information and metadata about the service such as which layers are published, what fields are included, and more.

9. Save your HTML file and run it: `http://arcgismachine/mybestaurants.html`. You should get a view similar to the following screenshot. Try using the map, scroll up and down to zoom in and zoom out. You can also use the plus and minus signs to perform the same action.

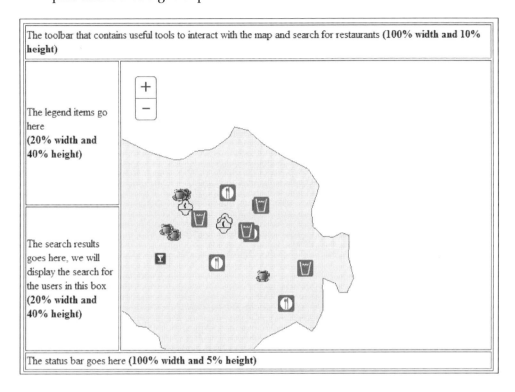

The final HTML file with the map can be found with the supporting files at `2955OT_02_Files\Code\bestaurants02_withmap.html`. You can also remove the alert message since we don't require it any more.

Note that when you zoom in, you will start getting the labels of the restaurants. These properties were already configured in the map document that was covered in *Publishing service in ArcGIS for Server* section in *Chapter 1, The Bestaurants Project*.

Customizing basic features

In this section, we will learn how to add and configure some basic features to our new map that will help our map get richer.

Default extent

The extent is a boundary of a map that limits what the users see. By default, when you publish a service, the current extent in your data gets saved in the service. That is why when you added the map to our application, we got a partial view and we had to zoom out to see all other restaurants. You will see that sometimes you will need to change the default extent, for instance, when your users want to see the full extent of the country, or sometimes each user wants to zoom to their working area when they run the application. In this section, we will learn how to change the default extent. We want to set the extent of our map to `-88.27`, `17.47`, `-88.16`, and `17.54`, which represents the center of Belize city:

1. Open the `mybestaurants.html` file with Notepad ++ if it is not already opened. Since the extent is a set of points, it is required to be identified with a spatial reference. A spatial reference is a projection which helps ArcGIS identify a point. The default spatial reference for our data has a **WKID (Well-Known-ID)** of `4326`. You can get the list of spatial references at `http://spatialreference.org/ref/esri/`. My book *Learning ArcGIS Geodatabase*, published by *Packt Publishing*, talks in detail about spatial references. Add the following code to create a spatial reference object:

```
...
function startup() {
  //create the spatial reference object.
  var sr = new esri.SpatialReference({wkid:4326});
  //create the map object and load it into the 'mymap'
  var map = new esri.Map("mymap")
...
```

2. Next, we need to create the extent object and pass coordinates of the upper left point and the lower right point for our extent. Then we pass the spatial reference object to the extent. Add the following code to your file:

```
...
function startup() {
  //create the spatial reference object.
  var sr = new esri.SpatialReference({wkid:4326});

  //create the extent object.
  var startExtent = new esri.geometry.Extent(-88.27, 17.47,
    -88.16, 17.54, sr);
  //create the map object and load it into the 'mymap'
  var map = new esri.Map("mymap")
...
```

3. Finally, we have to load our map with the new extent, which will force our map to load in that extent. For that we will modify the new `esri.Map` and add some parameters as follows.

```
...
function startup() {
  //create the spatial reference object.
  var sr = new esri.SpatialReference({wkid:4326});
  //create the extent object
  var startExtent = new esri.geometry.Extent(-88.27, 17.47,
    -88.16, 17.54, sr);
  //create the map object and load it into the 'mymap'
  var map = new esri.Map
  (
    "mymap",
    {
      extent: startExtent
    }
  );
...
```

4. Save and run your new updated web application under `http://arcgismachine/mybestaurants.html`. You should see the updated map as shown in the following screenshot. Notice how the full map is shown. You may find the final file under `2955OT_02_Files\Code\bestaurants03_withextent.html`.

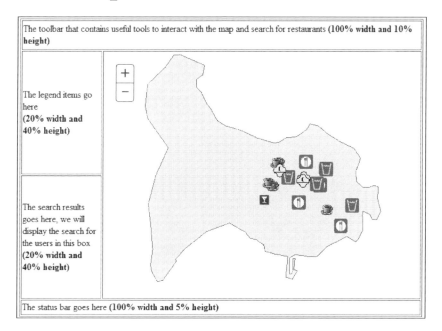

Adding the legend

We have set the default extent for the map, so now it is time to add the legend, which will show us the different types of restaurants in the map. The legend can be fetched from the same service that we are consuming. Adding the legend is simple. First we will need to add the div element where the legend will be generated, and we know where that is. Secondly, we create a legend by passing the layer object and then provide the location where it will generate. Follow these steps to add the legend.

1. Edit your `mybestaurants.html` file and replace the text under the `<!-- The legend of the map goes here -->` tag with the following `div` element:

   ```
   ...
   <tr>
     <td width='20%' height ='40%'>
       <!-- The legend of the map goes here -->
       <div id = 'mylegend'>
       </div>
     </td>
     <td width='80%' height ='85%' rowspan =2 valign = top>
       <div id='mymap' class='arcgismap' >
       </div>
     </td>
   </tr>
   ...
   ```

2. Since the `Legend` object is located in another library, we need to reference that library. Add `dojo.require("esri.dijit.Legend")` as follows:

   ```
   ...
   <script>
     dojo.require("esri.map");
     dojo.require("esri.dijit.Legend");
     function startup()
     {
       //create the spatial reference object.
       var sr = new esri.SpatialReference({wkid:4326});
   ...
   ```

3. In the `startup` function, create the legend object and pass the map and the div element where the legend will be placed. Calling `legend.startup` will show the legend:

   ```
   //create the map object and load it into the 'mymap' div element
   var map = new esri.Map("mymap", { extent: startExtent } );
   //load the layer into an object
   ```

```
var lyr = new esri.layers.ArcGISDynamicMapServiceLayer
  ( "http://arcgismachine:6080/arcgis/rest/services
  /Bestaurants/MapServer"
);
//add the legend
var legend = new esri.dijit.Legend({map:map}, "mylegend");
legend.startup();
//add the layer to map
map.addLayer(lyr);
...
```

Try running your web application using `http://arcgismachine/mybestaurants.html`. You should get the legend on the place we want it to show as displayed in the following screenshot. You may find the final updated file at `2955OT_02_Files\Code\bestaurants04_withlegend.html`.

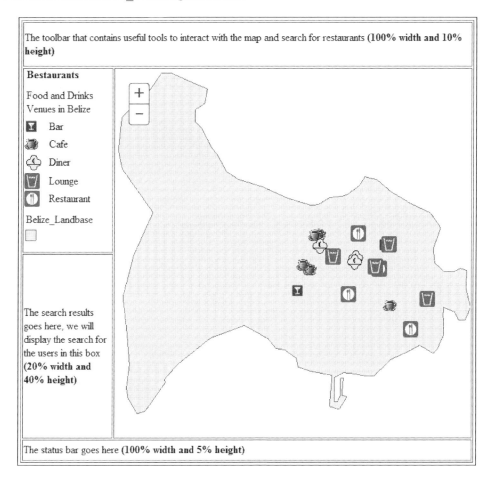

Summary

In this chapter, we created a basic ArcGIS web application. We installed and configured the IIS web server and created a basic web application. Then we dove through the ArcGIS JavaScript API where we learned how to add a map and load a service. We then customized the map to modify the default extent and add the legend.

In the next chapter, we will work more with advanced function of the ArcGIS JavaScript API to query the Bestaurants service and retrieve information.

3
Querying ArcGIS Services

So far, we have managed to create a basic ArcGIS web application. We started by installing and configuring the web server and setting up the basic HTML code. Then, we learned to write some ArcGIS JavaScript code to communicate with ArcGIS services. We added a map object and loaded a *dynamic service* into the map. Then, we customized the default extent of the map and added a legend to view the map. However, our Bestaurants web application is still far from finished. We need to implement the rest of the functionalities requested by the project.

In this chapter, we will learn how to query ArcGIS services to retrieve and display data. We will learn the concept of the feature layers, where we will use it to query and retrieve data, and to identify features. Then we will learn to use the definition query to filter the results, and finally, we will write the search function and display the results, which can be later used with the map.

 Dynamic map service: This is a service which when requested pulls out the latest data from the database ensuring real-time updates. However, it is expensive to call in terms of response time as it requires contact to the database every time a call is made.

Feature layers

In the previous chapters, we introduced the Dynamic map service object. That object was easy to use and implement since it takes care of everything from the symbology, scaling, labeling, and layer grouping. It fetches all the layers in your service and adds them to the map. The disadvantage of Dynamic map service layer is that it doesn't allow you to interact with the individual sub-layers in a convenient way. You can't loop through the sub-layers to fetch individual layers; therefore you cannot, of course, query the layers. Dynamic map services are mainly used for representation. That is why we will replace it with the **feature layer** as we will see in the next section.

Feature layer: This is a layer, which allows read access to the individual ArcGIS records in the corresponding table and accepts user queries.

Adding feature layers

As we have learned in the previous chapters, our service contains two layers, **Food and Drinks**, and **Belize Landbase**. This dynamic layer is just for representation, we used it to display our work. We will need to create two feature layers to replace the single dynamic map service layer so that we can unlock more functionality.

Don't worry if you didn't complete *Chapter 1, The Bestaurants Project,* or *Chapter 2, Setting Up the Basic Web Application*, the latest files and documents are available for you to use.

Follow these steps to add the feature layers:

1. You can continue from your previous `mybestaurants.html` file from *Chapter 2, Setting Up the Basic Web Application*. You can also get the same file from `29550T_03_Files\Code\bestaurants01_basicmap.html`, copy it to `c:\inetpub\wwwroot`, and rename it to `mybestaurants.html`.

2. We will now learn how to get the direct layer URL, which we will use to create the feature layer. Open this URL in your browser `http://arcgismachine:6080/arcgis/rest/services/Bestaurants/MapServer`. You will see that each layer has a number, which uniquely identifies the layer. This is illustrated in the following screenshot:

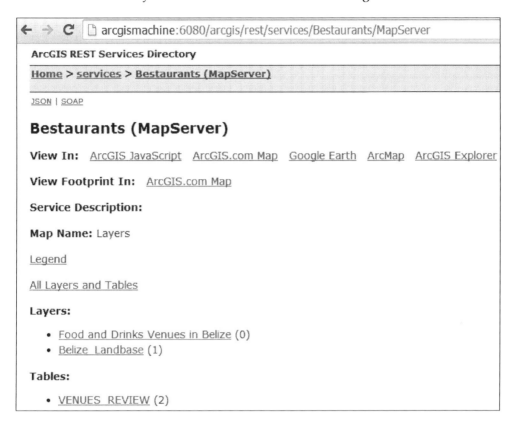

Each ID can be appended to the service URL to point directly to that layer. The layer ID is determined by the order of the layers in the map document (mxd). This is useful to create the feature layer. In this case, our food and drinks layer's ID value is 0 and landbase's ID value is 1, and there is one table that contains the reviews, which we will be using in *Chapter 4, Rich Content and Mobile Integration*, with the ID value 2.

3. Edit `mybestaurants.html` with Notepad++. We will start by adding the reference to the feature layer as you can see in the following code:

```
...
<script>
  dojo.require("esri.map");
  dojo.require("esri.layers.featurelayer");
  dojo.require("esri.dijit.Legend");
  function startup()
  {
...
```

4. Now, we will add `food and drinks` and `landbase` as different layers. The URLs, as you might have guessed, will be `http://arcgismachine:6080/arcgis/rest/services/Bestaurants/MapServer/0` for food and drinks and `http://arcgismachine:6080/arcgis/rest/services/Bestaurants/MapServer/1` for landbase. Add the following code:

```
...
//create the map object and load it into the 'mymap' div element
var map = new esri.Map ("mymap", { extent: startExtent } );
//load the food and drinks layer into an object
var lyr_foodanddrinks = new esri.layers.FeatureLayer
  ("http://arcgismachine:6080/arcgis/rest/services
  /Bestaurants/MapServer/0", { outFields: ["*"] } );

//load the landbase layer into an object
var lyr_landbase = new esri.layers.FeatureLayer
(
  "http://arcgismachine:6080/arcgis/rest/services
    /Bestaurants/MapServer/1", { outFields: ["*"] }
);
//add the legend
var legend = new esri.dijit.Legend({map:map}, "mylegend");
legend.startup();
...
```

Notice that we have added a new parameter while creating the feature layer object; this will specify what fields (and consequently, the values in those fields) will be returned with the objects. We have specified the "*" keyword, which will return all fields. It is not good practice to return all fields as it affects the performance since the server has to return all of the data for all fields; plus it affects security as someone can sniff your data and see through all the information that was passed. However, for simplicity, we will do so.

5. Now, we need to add the two layers to the map to display. Add the following code to your file:

```
...
//add the legend
var legend = new esri.dijit.Legend({map:map}, "mylegend");
legend.startup();
//add the layers to map
map.addLayer(lyr_landbase);
map.addLayer(lyr_foodanddrinks);
...
```

6. We will need to do some changes in the interface design. Since we have added each layer separately, the legend got bigger, so we need to increase the size of the legend cell from 40 percent to 50 percent and shrink the results cell to 30 percent, so add the following code:

```
...
<tr>
  <td width='20%' height ='50%'>
    <!-- The legend of the map goes here -->
    <div id = 'mylegend'>
    </div>
  </td>
  <td width='80%' height ='85%' rowspan =2 valign = top>
    <div id='mymap' class='arcgismap' >
    </div>
  </td>
</tr>
<tr>
  <td width='20%' height ='30%'>
    <!-- The search results will go here -->
    The search results goes here, we will display the search for
the users in this box <br> <b>(20% width and 30% height)</b>
  </td>
</tr>
...
```

7. Save the `mybestaurants.html` file and run the application `http://arcgismachine/mybestaurants.html` to make sure you still get the map as you can see in the following screenshot. You can find the updated file at `2955OT_03_Files\Code\bestaurants02_featurelayer.html`.

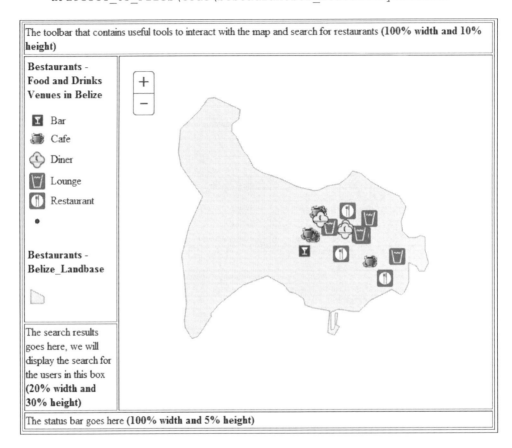

Identifying restaurants

Now that we have added the feature layers, we can do our first query to identify the restaurants when you click on the map. The identify function is relatively easy to implement; all we need is the object `InfoTemplate`, which will display a pop up window when the user clicks on a restaurant. You can guess that this will be applied on the **food_and_drinks** layer and not on the **landbase** layer since this is where our data will be held. You can read more about the `InfoTemplate` object at `https://developers.arcgis.com/javascript/jsapi/infotemplate-amd.html`.

Fortunately, the `InfoTemplate` object allows us to create our own HTML result dialog box. We can display the field values by adding `${FIELD_NAME}`, where `FIELD_NAME` is the name of the column that is to be displayed. This will be understood and converted into a corresponding value by `InfoTemplate` as explained in the following steps:

1. Edit the `mybestaurants.html` file; first, we will create a string `t`, where we will save our desired HTML result. We will then create an `InfoTemplate` object and pass the HTML code. Finally, we will assign the `InfoTemplate` object to the layer that is supposed to be identified. Add the following code to your file:

```
...
//load the food and drinks layer into an object
var lyr_foodanddrinks = new esri.layers.FeatureLayer
  ("http://arcgismachine:6080/arcgis/rest/services
    /Bestaurants/MapServer/0", { outFields: ["*"] } );
  //identify restaurant and display the name and the rating
  var t = "<b>${NAME}</b> [${RATING}/5]<br>" +
    "${WEBSITE}<br>" + "${DESCRIPTION}";
  //create the info template object and pass the template
  var infoTemplate = new esri.InfoTemplate("Identify",t);
  //assign the infotemplate so it applies on every feature in this
layer
  lyr_foodanddrinks.setInfoTemplate(infoTemplate);
//load the landbase layer into an object
  var lyr_landbase = new esri.layers.FeatureLayer
    ("http://arcgismachine:6080/arcgis/rest/services
    /Bestaurants/MapServer/1", { =outFields: ["*"] } );
...
```

2. Save the file and run your application. Test it by clicking on the restaurants. You can see the **Identify** dialog box shows the name, rating (out of **5**), the website, and some description about the restaurant as shown in the following screenshot:

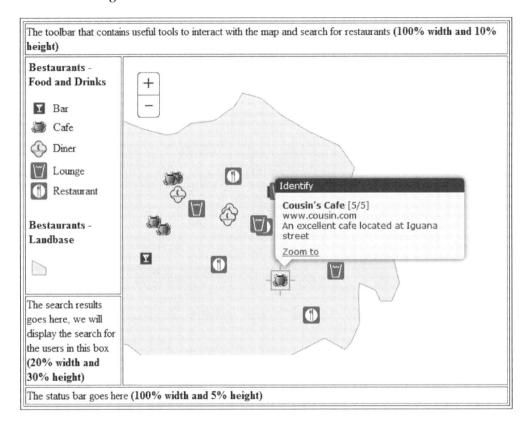

You just added the identify restaurant function, which will prove really useful for your users! You can find the latest code at 2955OT_03_Files\Code\ bestaurants03_identify.html.

Using definition query to filter map

After we have added the identify feature on our web application, it is time to add some filters. We will start by filtering the map by category and rating. The user will select a category, say the **Café** category, and the map should be updated to show only café. This is where we will use the upper toolbar.

Filtering by category

First, we will need to add the necessary control for the filter that will assist the user to a query. If you referred to our interface design that was covered in *Chapter 1, The Bestaurants Project*, you will notice that we can use a drop-down list for the categories and as the user changes; we will update our feature layer.

As a programmer, you should know that if we are planning to make changes to an object on runtime, it should be set as modular and that's what we will do. This can be achieved by moving the var lyr_foodanddrinks variable above the startup function and update the assignment.

> lyr_foodanddrinks is a global scope variable and it will be used in all the functions. We will be using global variables in this book for simplicity reasons. The best practice is to pass the variables in the function as we need them, or even better, use object-oriented approaches. This will make the code harder to read but definitely more robust and reusable.

Follow these steps to add the filter by category:

1. Edit the mybestaurants.html file and make the following changes to your code. Note that we have removed the var keyword in the assignment; this has been done to avoid shadowing:

```
dojo.require("esri.map");
dojo.require("esri.layers.featurelayer");
dojo.require("esri.dijit.Legend");
var lyr_foodanddrinks;
function startup()
{
  //create the spatial reference object.
  …

  …

  lyr_foodanddrinks = new esri.layers.FeatureLayer
    ("http://arcgismachine:6080/arcgis/rest/services
    /Bestaurants/MapServer/0", { outFields: ["*"] } );
```

2. Next, find the `<!-- The toolbar where we will place tools -->` tag and replace the content with a drop-down box containing the five categories. Each category has a number and I have included these numbers as the values for each option as follows. Note that I used code `99`, which doesn't exist for all the categories; we will cover how I manipulate this later.

```
...
<tr>
  <td colspan =2 width='100%' height ='10%'>
    <!-- The toolbar where we will place tools -->
    <select id = 'cmbcategories' >
      <option value = "99" selected>All</option>
      <option value = "0">Diner</option>
      <option value = "1">Restaurant</option>
      <option value = "2">Cafe</option>
      <option value = "4">Lounge</option>
      <option value = "3">Bar</option>
    </select>
  </td>
</tr>
...
```

3. We now have to add an event on this drop-down box so that when the user changes the value, a function will be called as shown in the following code:

```
...
<tr>
  <td colspan =2 width='100%' height ='10%'>
    <!-- The toolbar where we will place tools -->
    <select id = 'cmbcategories' onchange =
      'oncategorychange()'>
      <option value = "99" selected>All</option>
      <option value = "0">Diner</option>
      <option value = "1">Restaurant</option>
      <option value = "2">Cafe</option>
      <option value = "4">Lounge</option>
      <option value = "3">Bar</option>
    </select>
  </td>
</tr>
...
```

Adding a new category will force us to update the code here as well. As you progress through the book, you will be able to query the categories and populate them dynamically.

4. We will add the function `oncategorychange()` just after `dojo.addOnLoad(startup)`. The function should get the new value of the drop-down list as shown in the following code:

```
...
dojo.addOnLoad(startup);
function oncategorychange()
{
  c = document.getElementById('cmbcategories').value;


}
</script>
...
```

5. We will make the change we promised on the feature layer, which is to set the definition expression and pass a filter as `Category = value`. Write the following code in your function:

```
...
dojo.addOnLoad(startup);
  function oncategorychange()
  {
    c = document.getElementById('cmbcategories').value;
    lyr_foodanddrinks.setDefinitionExpression("CATEGORY="+c);
  }
</script>
...
```

That's it, now save your file and run it at http://arcgismachine/mybestaurants.html. You should see the map updating as you change the drop-down list as illustrated in the following screenshot:

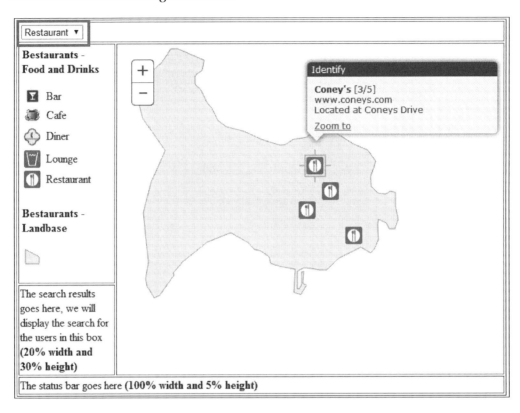

We will add one final code, where when the user selects All, the filter should be cleared. A simple if statement will do the trick as shown in the following code:

```
...
function oncategorychange()
{
  c = document.getElementById('cmbcategories').value;
  if (c == 99)
    lyr_foodanddrinks.setDefinitionExpression("");
  else
    lyr_foodanddrinks.setDefinitionExpression("CATEGORY="+c);
}
...
```

You can find the final category filter code under 29550T_03_Files\Code\bestaurants04_categoryfilter.html.

Filtering by rating

Similarly, we can use the same approach to filter our restaurants by their rating. This will allow the users, for instance, to see only restaurants which have an excellent rating. Like what we did with the category filtering, we need to add the necessary design HTML tags. Follow these steps:

1. Edit `mybestaurants.html` and add the following drop-down list control. Similar to the previous event, we will call the `onratingchange` function, which we will add later as shown in the following code:

```
<!-- The toolbar where we will place tools -->
Category <select id = 'cmbcategories' onchange =
  'oncategorychange()'>
  <option value = "99" selected>All</option>
  <option value = "0">Diner</option>
  <option value = "1">Restaurant</option>
  <option value = "2">Cafe</option>
  <option value = "4">Lounge</option>
  <option value = "3">Bar</option>
  </select>
  Rating <select id = 'cmbrating' onchange =
    'onratingchange()'>
  <option value = "99" selected>All</option>
  <option value = "1">Poor</option>
  <option value = "2">Fair</option>
  <option value = "3">Average</option>
  <option value = "4">Good</option>
  <option value = "5">Excellent</option>
</select>
...
```

2. Next, we will add the function `onratingchange`; note it will look almost like `oncategorychange` except for the field name shown in the following code:

```
...
function onratingchange()
{
  c = document.getElementById('cmbrating').value;
  if (c == 99)
    lyr_foodanddrinks.setDefinitionExpression("");
  else
    lyr_foodanddrinks.setDefinitionExpression("RATING = " + c);
}
...
```

3. You can save and run your application; however, there is a small logical bug that we need to address. The filters, category, and rating work great independently, but when you combine them together, you don't get the correct result. That is what we will need to fix, the application has to remember each choice in a modular variable. I have taken care of this logic for you with a little JavaScript code. I have added a new function `filterlayer` that will be called every time the category or the rating changes. Take a look at the following code:

```
...
dojo.addOnLoad(startup);
var selected_category = 99;
var selected_rating =99;

function oncategorychange()
{
  c = document.getElementById('cmbcategories').value;
  selected_category = c;
  //call the filter
filterlayer();
}

function onratingchange()
{
  c = document.getElementById('cmbrating').value;
  selected_rating = c;
  //call the filter
  filterlayer();
}

function filterlayer()
{
  var q = "1 = 1";
  if (selected_category != 99)
    q = q + " AND CATEGORY = " + selected_category;
  if (selected_rating != 99)
    q = q + " AND RATING = " + selected_rating;
    lyr_foodanddrinks.setDefinitionExpression(q);
}
...
```

Save your file and test it. Your application should now work correctly. Consult the following screenshot for verification. You can find the latest code at `29550T_03_Files\Code\bestaurants05_ratingfilter.html`.

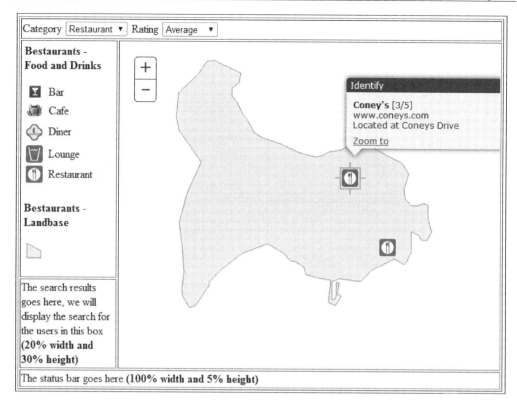

Searching and displaying restaurants by name

We have completed the feature layer filtering, where we learned how to use the layer definition to filter out map results. However, there are cases where we will need to get the results, manipulate them, list, and interact with them. This is where we will use the query tasks. In this section, we will learn how to search restaurants by name and display the results and then we will add some code to the result to interact with the map.

However, first, we need to learn about an important object that is the center of ArcGIS JavaScript development and that is **feature**.

Feature: This is an object that represents a single record in a feature layer. Feature has a list of attributes and a geometry that represents the location of that feature. A geometry can mainly be a point, line, or a polygon.

Each feature has a geometry; we use that geometry to highlight and zoom to the feature on a map. Beside geometry, feature has a list of attributes; the attributes can be accessed by using the following code:

```
Feature.attributes["FIELD_NAME"]
```

where FIELD_NAME is the field or attribute you want to return the value of. For example, take a look at the following piece of code. This will retrieve the name field in the feature:

```
var name = Feature.attributes['name'];
```

One of the methods using which a feature can be obtained is by using the query object; this is what we will learn in the next section. Keep reading!

Displaying the query results

We will write a logic where the user can type in a restaurant name (or part of it) and then display the results in the results box that we saved all this time. Follow these steps:

1. Edit the mybestaurants.html file and add a textbox control where the user will be typing the restaurant name and a button that the user will click to execute the query by calling the executequery function that we will write. Add the following code in the toolbar:

```
...
Rating <select id = 'cmbrating' onchange =
   'onratingchange()'>
   <option value = "99" selected>All</option>
   <option value = "1">Poor</option>
   <option value = "2">Fair</option>
   <option value = "3">Average</option>
   <option value = "4">Good</option>
   <option value = "5">Excellent</option>
</select>
Name <input type = 'text' id = 'txtq'> <input type = 'button'
   value = 'Search' onclick = 'executequery()'>
...
```

2. The query object requires a specialist library to reference, and a modular variable to declare so that we can use it in our `executequery` function. Add the following code by resetting the required statements:

```
...
<script>
  dojo.require("esri.map");
  dojo.require("esri.layers.featurelayer");
  dojo.require("esri.dijit.Legend");
  dojo.require("esri.tasks.query");
  var queryTask;
  var lyr_foodanddrinks;
  function startup()
{
  ...
```

3. Now, just before the end of the `startup` function, add the following code to create the `querytask` object that points to our feature `food_and_drinks` layer layer 0:

```
//add the layer to map
map.addLayer(lyr_landbase);
map.addLayer(lyr_foodanddrinks);
//Create query task
queryTask = new esri.tasks.QueryTask
(
  "http://arcgismachine:6080/arcgis/rest/services/
    Bestaurants/MapServer/0"
);
```

4. Create the `executequery` function. This function will get the current value of the textbox, create a query object, set the text property, sets the output fields, and then passes the query object to `queryTask`. The `queryTask.execute` takes the query object, finds all matching results, and returns them to a parameter function. In this case, the returning function is `showResults`. We haven't created this function yet but we will look at this in the coming pages:

```
...
function executequery()
{
  q = document.getElementById('txtq').value;
  var query = new esri.tasks.Query();
  query.outFields = ["NAME", "RATING"];
  query.text = q;
```

```
        queryTask.execute(query, showResults);
}
...
```

5. Let's make some space for the result and add the following element under
    the `<!-- The search results will go here -->` tag. Also add `valign`
    `=top` so that the results snap to the top instead of floating in the center:

```
...
<tr>
  <td width='20%' height ='30%' valign = top>
    <!-- The search results will go here -->
    <div id = 'myresults'>
    </div>
  </td>
</tr>
...
```

6. Let's work on our `showResults` function. This function accepts the parameter
    `results`, which is an array of features passed in by `queryTask`. The `results`
    object contains an array of features. A feature describes a single record, in our
    case, it is a restaurant. The feature object has an array of attributes that can be
    used to get the value of each field. Add the following `showResults` function
    to your code:

```
function showResults (results)
{
    //we are going to build our result html string
    var resulthtml = "";
    var resultCount = results.features.length;
    for (var i = 0; i < resultCount; i++)
    {
        //for each single feature or record in the result
        var feature = results.features[i];

    }
}
...
```

7. Now, we need to get each single record, get the NAME and RATING values and
    write them to the `resulthtml` string as shown in the following code:

```
function showResults (results)
{
    //we are going to build our result html string
    var resulthtml = "";
```

```
  var resultCount = results.features.length;
  for (var i = 0; i < resultCount; i++)
   {
     //for each single feature or record in the result
     var feature = results.features[i];

     //display the name
     resulthtml = resulthtml + "<b>Name:</b> " +
       feature.attributes["NAME"] + "<Br>";
     //display the reating
     resulthtml = resulthtml + "<b>Rating:</b> " +
       feature.attributes["RATING"];
     //new line
     resulthtml = resulthtml + "<br><br>";

   }
}
```

8. Finally, we have to show the results in the element; this is done after the loop as shown here:

```
function showResults (results)
{
  //we are going to build our result html string
  var resulthtml = "";
  var resultCount = results.features.length;
  for (var i = 0; i < resultCount; i++)
  {
    //for each single feature or record in the result
    var feature = results.features[i];

    //display the name
    resulthtml = resulthtml + "<b>Name:</b> " +
      feature.attributes["NAME"] + "<Br>";
    //display the reating
    resulthtml = resulthtml + "<b>Rating:</b> " +
      feature.attributes["RATING"];
    //new line
    resulthtml = resulthtml + "<br><br>";

  }
  //add the results to myresults element.
  document.getElementById("myresults").innerHTML = resulthtml;

}
```

9. Save your code and run your application, type `Mercy` in the textbox and click on **search**. You should get two results as shown in the following screenshot, one with a **Rating** of **4** and one with a **Rating** of **5**. We will work in the coming chapters to enhance the view and display stars instead of a number. If you know how to develop it properly with JavaScript, you can do it as well. You can find the latest working code with the query at `29550T_03_ Files\Code\bestaurants06_query.html`.

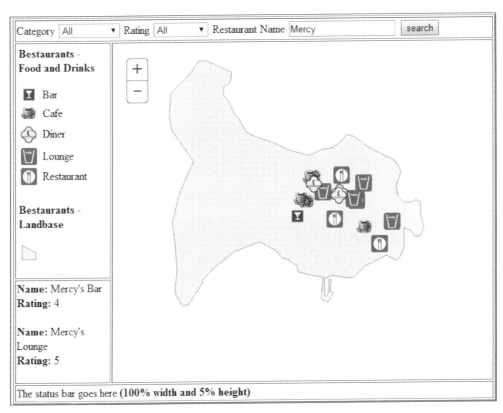

Note that the query is case sensitive. We can make searches not case sensitive by using specific database SQL commands such as UPPER() and LOWER(). See this link for more details: `http://qr.net/sqlupper`.

Interacting with the results to highlight the map

Interacting with the map requires having an extra parameter fetched from the query, and that is geometry. Geometry is an expensive attribute to query for, and that is why you should enable it only when you really need it. To enable retrieving geometry, we have to set the `returnGeometry` value to `true` in the query object as covered in the following steps:

1. Edit your `mybestaurants.html` file and add the following line to the `executequery` function; this way we can have the geometry object in our feature:

```
...
function executequery()
{
  q = document.getElementById('txtq').value;
  var query = new esri.tasks.Query();
  query.returnGeometry = true;
  query.outFields = ["NAME", "RATING"];
  query.text = q;
  queryTask.execute(query, showResults);
}
...
```

2. To link the results of the query to the map, we should first save the results so that it is accessible. We also need to make the map a modular variable since we will use it at other places. Make sure that you remove `var map` from the `startup` function and just replace it with a map to avoid shadowing as shown here:

```
...
var queryTask;
var lyr_foodanddrinks;
var queryresults;
var map;
function startup()
{
...
```

Create the map object and load it into the `mymap` div element:

```
map = new esri.Map("mymap", { extent: startExtent } );
...
```

3. In the `showResults` function, we need to save a copy of the results in the `queryresults` modular variables as shown in the following code:

```
...
function showResults (results)
{
  //save a copy of the results
  queryresults = results;
//we are going to build our result html string
  var resulthtml = ""
  var resultCount = results.features.length;
...
```

4. Now, we need to modify the `Name` value so that it will be interactive, an anchor element will do the trick. When the user clicks on the name, a function `showRestaurant` will be called, and the index of the record will be passed to that function. This way the function can retrieve the feature by its index. Add the following code in the `showResults` function:

```
...
for (var i = 0; i < resultCount; i++)
  {
    //for each single feature or record in the result var
    feature = results.features[i];
    //display the name with a hyperlink to zoom to the map
    resulthtml = resulthtml + "<b>Name:</b> <a href='#' onclick
      = 'showRestaurant(" + i + ")'>" +
      feature.attributes["NAME"] + "</a><Br>";
    //display the reating
    resulthtml = resulthtml + "<b>Rating:</b> " +
      feature.attributes["RATING"];
    //new line
    resulthtml = resulthtml + "<br><br>";
}
...
```

5. Of course, `showRestaurant` doesn't exist, so we have to write it. Add the `showRestaurant` function and make it accept an integer, which will be the index. We will use this index and `queryresults` to point to the very feature that the user has clicked on. Then we will highlight the restaurant on the map with a special object called `symbol`. The `symbol` object can be styled, colored, and assigned to features to be displayed on the map as shown in the following code:

```
...
function showRestaurant(i)
{
```

```
  //get the clicked feature
  var feature = queryresults.features[i];
//mark up symbol are for points.
Var symbol = new esri.symbol.SimpleMarkerSymbol();
//set the size
symbol.setSize(50);
//and the color (yellow) and transparency of 50% (0.5)
symbol.setColor(new dojo.Color([255,255,0,0.5]));
...
//finally set the symbol to the record
feature.setSymbol(symbol);
}
...
```

6. After we set the symbol to our feature, we can add that record to the map as a graphic. However, we first have to clear the map from all previous graphics so that we don't get duplicates. Add the following code to do so:

```
...
function showRestaurant(i)
{
  //get the clicked feature
  var feature = queryresults.features[i];
//mark up symbol are for points.
  Var symbol = new esri.symbol.SimpleMarkerSymbol();
  //set the size of the symbol
  symbol.setSize(50);
  //and the color (yellow) and transparency of 50% (0.5)
  symbol.setColor(new dojo.Color([255,255,0,0.5]));

  //finally set the symbol to the record
  feature.setSymbol(symbol);
  //clear any graphics on the map
  map.graphics.clear();
  //so we only add this one
  map.graphics.add(feature);
}
...
```

You have successfully completed the query functionalities. We have a working search engine for the Bestaurants project. Type a restaurant name and click on it. Take a look at the following screenshot for illustrations. You can find the final code for the application at `29550T_03_Files\Code\bestaurants07_queryhighlight.html`.

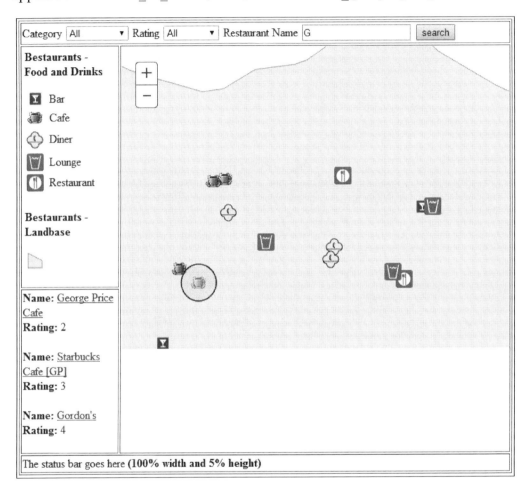

Summary

This chapter was filled with rich ArcGIS code. You have learned and used numerous new objects and functions in your Bestaurants web application. We have started with the concept of feature layer, which proved to be useful for creating our first tool: the identify tool. Then we used it to filter the map results by specifying a feature layer definition. We added the category and rating filters, and then we enriched our application by adding a search textbox. We used the textbox to send a query to the service, parsed the returning results, and displayed them on the page. Finally, we added the functionality of being able to interact with the map and highlight the result when the user clicks on a restaurant.

In the next chapter, we will enhance our web experience by adding more information to the restaurants results such as the review and the name of the user, which will add a nice touch to the application.

4
Rich Content and
Mobile Integration

Our Bestaurants web application is coming in to shape. We have developed and added a lot of functionalities to the application; we started with a simple HTML skeleton, added the map, and interacted with the map with some tools and queries. We have reached the stage where we can add rich content to the application, content that is not as easily accessible. The restaurants layer contains some good attributes that we have used to display such as name, description, website, and rating. However, the reviews and pictures for each restaurant are stored in other tables.

We are half way through the completion of our project where we acquired solid skills in ArcGIS web development. In this chapter, we will dive deeper and learn how to query and fetch this related data and display them consistently in our application so that it becomes more appealing to the tourist users.

Brief introduction to relationships

We will start by learning about relationships. A relationship is the key property of any relational database that is where the relational database management system got its name from. ArcGIS uses a relational model which means we have to deal with relationships in our coding.

Take a moment and review the database model back in *Chapter 1, The Bestaurants Project.* In the Bestaurants scenario, our `food_and_drinks` layer is related to another table called **VENUES_REVIEW**. Each relationship has a unique identifier that we will use to query the related records. Open the `food_and_drinks` layer by visiting the link: `http://arcgismachine:6080/arcgis/rest/services/Bestaurants/MapServer/0` and then scroll down to **Relationships** as you can see in the following screenshot:

Relationships:

- VENUES_REVIEW (0) -- *Related To*: VENUES_REVIEW (2)

Supported Operations:　Query　Query Related Records　Generate Renderer　Return Updates

Any relationship is composited of a primary key, which resides in the main or the source table. In our case it is `food_and_drinks`, and a foreign key that can be found in the destination table, `Venues_reviews`. The primary key of `food_and_drinks` is an autogenerated number by ArcGIS referred to as `ObjectID`, which is also the foreign key on the `Venues_reviews` table. So, we now know that to find the reviews for a restaurant feature *f*, we have to get the object ID of that *f*. We will learn how to do that in the following example.

 The **ObjectID** is a numeric number, which uniquely identifies any ArcGIS table or class and functions as a primary key for this table.

So how do I see the fields in the **VENUES_REVIEW** table? You can guess that it will have a unique URL just like the `food_and_drinks` table. Click on **VENUES_REVIEW (2)** to open the review table or simply open the page. The **VENUES_REVIEW** table has an ID of **2** while the relationship between them has an ID of **0**. It is important not to confuse the two. Take a look at the reviews table in the following screenshot:

Fields:

- OBJECTID *(type: esriFieldTypeOID , alias: OBJECTID)*
- REVIEW *(type: esriFieldTypeString , alias: Review , length: 3000)*
- REVIEW_DATE *(type: esriFieldTypeDate , alias: REVIEW_DATE , length: 8)*
- VENUE_OBJECTID *(type: esriFieldTypeInteger , alias: VENUE_OBJECTID)*
- USER *(type: esriFieldTypeString , alias: USER , length: 50)*
- RATING *(type: esriFieldTypeSmallInteger , alias: RATING)*

Relationships:

- Food_and_Drinks (0) -- *Related To*: Food and Drinks (0)

A simple relationship query example

Before diving into the actual implementation of our proposed interface design, which was to display the reviews in the results panel, we will work with a smaller example to understand how relationship queries work. In the following example, we will demonstrate how to get the review text and the name of the review user and display them in an alert message when the user clicks on a restaurant result:

1. You can continue from your previous `mybestaurants.html` file from *Chapter 3, Querying ArcGIS Services*. You can also get the same file from `29550T_03_Files\Code\bestaurants07_queryhighlight`, copy it to `c:\inetpub\wwwroot`, and rename it to `mybestaurants.html`.

2. First of all, the relationship query object that we will be using is located in a different library that we have to refer to. Add the following reference to your code:

```
...
<script>
  dojo.require("esri.map");
  dojo.require("esri.layers.featurelayer");
  dojo.require("esri.dijit.Legend");
  dojo.require("esri.tasks.query");
  dojo.require("esri.tasks.RelationshipQuery");
  function startup()
    {
...
```

3. Do you remember how we highlight a restaurant when a user clicks on the query result? We wrote a function called `showRestaurant`, and we will now go to that function and add some new code. We will first create a relationship query object, and then ask it to return all fields with `"*"` as done in the following code. Again, it is recommended to use the fields that you will absolutely require in your query for performance reasons. But, we will use `"*"` for simplicity:

```
//clear any graphics on the map
map.graphics.clear();
//so we only add this one
map.graphics.add(record);
//Create relationship query object
varrelatedReviews = new esri.tasks.RelationshipQuery();
//return all fields in the related table.
relatedReviews.outFields = ["*"];
...
```

4. We have to specify what the relationship ID is, which we saw in the previous screenshot. This is important for ArcGIS to be able to fetch that relationship metadata. Also, we have to give the `ObjectID` of the current clicked restaurant. Add the following code:

```
//Create relationship query object.
varrelatedReviews = new esri.tasks.RelationshipQuery();
//return all fields in the related table.
relatedReviews.outFields = ["*"];
//The relationship id is zero based on the url
relatedReviews.relationshipId = 0;
//get the object id
relatedReviews.objectIds = [record.attributes["OBJECTID"]];
...
```

5. This code will definitely generate an error. The reason is that we never asked the query to return the `ObjectID` field, we only asked for the name and the rating. We have to add the `ObjectID` field to our query fields. Go back to the `executequery` function and modify the code accordingly as shown in the following code snippet:

```
...
functionexecutequery()
{
  q = document.getElementById('txtq').value;
  var query = new esri.tasks.Query();
  query.returnGeometry = true;
  query.outFields = ["OBJECTID","NAME", "RATING"];
  query.text = q;
  queryTask.execute(query, showResults);
}
...
```

6. It is time to run our query. We always run a query on the feature layer by calling the `queryRelatedFeatures` function. We pass our relationship query object, and a function will be called when the query is completed. Let's call it `RelationQueryCompelete`. Add the following code:

```
//Create relationship query object
varrelatedReviews = new esri.tasks.RelationshipQuery();
//return all fields in the related table.
relatedReviews.outFields = ["*"];
//The relationship id is zero based on the url
```

```
relatedReviews.relationshipId = 0;
//get the object id
relatedReviews.objectIds = [record.attributes["OBJECTID"]];
//execute the query and then call the RelationQueryCompelete
lyr_foodanddrinks.queryRelatedFeatures
   (relatedReviews, RelationQueryCompelete);
...
```

7. Of course, we have to write our `RelationQueryCompelete` function; the function gives us a key-value pair array. The key is the object ID of the feature and the value is the actual related record. This, in our case, is the review. So, we have to loop through the records to get it. There might be more than one review for the same restaurant and you can loop through them and get them all. However, we are only interested in the first related record, `features[0]`. The related record can be treated as a feature without a geometry, still you can access the `attributes` property to get your attribute. We are interested in the REVIEW and USER fields. Add the following function to your code:

```
...
functionRelationQueryCompelete(relatedRecords)
{
  for (varoid in relatedRecords)
  {
    varfset = relatedRecords[oid];
    //get the first related record
    varfirstrecord = fset.features[0];
    var review = firstrecord.attributes["REVIEW"];
    var user = firstrecord.attributes["USER"];
    alert("By " + user + ": " + review);
  }
}
...
```

8. Save the `mybestaurants.html` file and run the application `http://arcgismachine/mybestaurants.html`. Do a search on `Mercy` and click on **Mercy's Bar**. You should get a pop up that says **By Walter White: Love this place!** as you can see in the following screenshot. This means our query has worked. You can find the updated file at `2955OT_04_Files\Code\bestaurants01_getrelationonclick.html`. This code is good even when there are no related records; the code will not enter the loop, and eventually won't show the results.

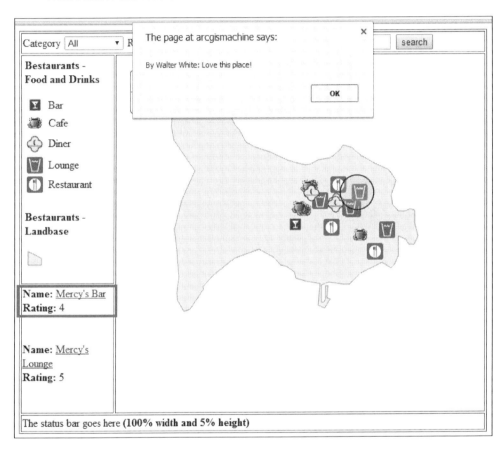

Working with Restaurants' rich content

We learned in the previous section to do a simple relation query when the user clicks on a result. It was quite simple, as it was only a single feature at a time. However, what is required from us is something different. We need to actually show these reviews as the result is displayed, hence we will be dealing with multiple features at the same time. Because of the *asynchronous* nature of our code, we cannot use the conventional method of querying and waiting for the result, because the code will be long executed and the last result will already be displayed before we can even get the related records of the first result.

 Asynchronous code is a piece of code that gets called by an initiator and is executed separately. The initiator does not wait for that code to be completed before resuming the rest of the code segments.

We will learn how to fix this in the next section.

Displaying reviews

We have to make some changes in the `ShowResults` function. This is the function that shows the query results and this is where we need to query for related records. While displaying the query result, we add a div element placeholder named by `object id` of the current feature. This will be our first step, as this way we have a review placeholder for each feature. Follow these steps to start displaying the reviews:

1. Edit the `mybestaurants.html` file and add the following code to `ShowResults`:

```
//display the name
resulthtml = resulthtml + "<b>Name:</b>
  <a href='#' onclick = 'showRestaurant(" + i + ")'
  >" + record.attributes["NAME"] + "</a><Br>";
//display the reating
resulthtml = resulthtml + "<b>Rating:</b> " +
  record.attributes["RATING"];
//create a place holder for each review to be populated later
resulthtml = resulthtml + "<div id = 'review" +
  record.attributes["OBJECTID"] + "'></div>";
//new line
resulthtml = resulthtml + "<br><br>";
```

2. We have marked the created div with the object ID, so we can access it later by simply specifying `"review"` + OBJECTID. Next, just before the end of ShowResults, call the AddReviews function and pass the same `results` object that got passed to ShowResults to it so that we can use it. This doesn't exist yet but we are going to add it in the following code snippet:

```
...
//add the results to myresults
element.document.getElementById("myresults").innerHTML =
    resulthtml;
}
AddReviews(results);
}// end of ShowResults
```

3. Next, add the AddReviews function, get the results, and create the basic loop. Use the ShowResults for preparation to query the related records. We will loop again on each result and send a query to get the related records:

```
...
functionAddReviews(results)
{
    varresultCount = results.features.length;
    for (vari = 0; i<resultCount; i++)
    {
        //for each single feature or record in the result
        var record = results.features[i];
        // Relationship query code goes here
    }
}
...
```

4. Next, we need to create a relationship query object; by now you know how to do it. Let the results go to RelationQueryComplete that we created at the beginning of the chapter:

```
...
functionAddReviews(results)
{
    varresultCount = results.features.length;
    for (vari = 0; i<resultCount; i++)
    {
    //for each single feature or record in the result
        var record = results.features[i];
        // Relationship query code goes here
        //Create relationship query object
        varrelatedReviews = new esri.tasks.RelationshipQuery();
```

```
    //return all fields in the related
    table.relatedReviews.outFields = ["*"];
    //The relationship id is zero based on the url
    relatedReviews.relationshipId = 0;
    //get the object id
    relatedReviews.objectIds = [record.attributes["OBJECTID"]];
    //execute the query and wait, the RelationQueryComplete
function will be called with the results once the query is
finished
    lyr_foodanddrinks.queryRelatedFeatures
       (relatedReviews, RelationQueryCompelete);


  }
}
...
```

5. The final change is in the `RelationQueryCompelete` function. We don't want to bug the user with alert messages, so instead we will simply update the corresponding review `div` object ID HTML tag. Fortunately, we have the object ID (`oid`) by looping through the key value pair in `relatedRecords`:

   ...

```
functionRelationQueryCompelete(relatedRecords)
{
  for (varoid in relatedRecords)
  {
    varfset = relatedRecords[oid];
    varfirstrecord = fset.features[0];
    var review = firstrecord.attributes["REVIEW"];
    var user = firstrecord.attributes["USER"];
    //update the div id with the review and the user
    document.getElementById("review" + oid).innerHTML = "By " +
      user + ": " + review;
  }
}
...
```

6. Let's style the review: make both the review and the user italic.

```
//update the div id with the review and the user
document.getElementById("review" + oid).innerHTML =
  "<i>" + review + "<br>-" + user + "</i>"
```

That's it. Save your file and run it `http://arcgismachine/mybestaurants.html`. You should see the reviews show up as you run the query. Run a query on **Mercy** as shown in the following screenshot:

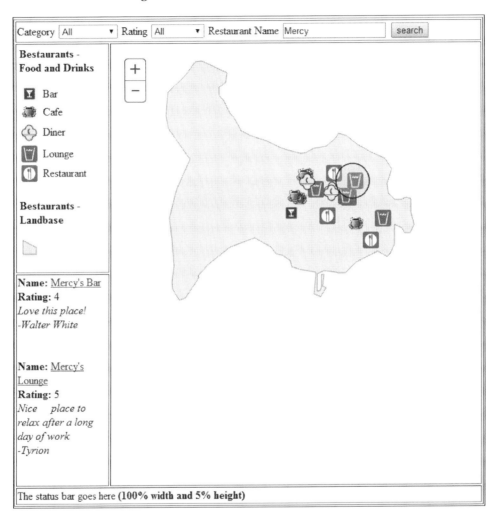

 You can find the final code at `2955OT_04_Files\Code\bestaurnts02_queryreviews.html` for displaying reviews.

Displaying pictures

Pictures of the restaurants are stored as attachments; the attachments are, in a way, related records; however, they are accessed in a much simpler method. Using the feature layer, we have to call the `queryAttachmentInfos` function, give it the object ID we want to retrieve the attachments for, and then parse the result in a separated function. Since it is an asynchronous call, we will use the same approach as the reviews; we will reserve some `div` elements for the restaurant pictures and display them after the result's load is completed.

The results will give us an attachment array. Each attachment has a `url` property that we are interested in to show a picture of that restaurant in the result. You can learn more about ArcGIS attachments at `http://qr.net/esriatt`. Follow these steps to start displaying the pictures:

1. Edit `mybestaurants.html`, go to the `showResults` function, and add a place holder `div` element for the pictures as we did to the reviews using the following code:

    ```
    //display the name
    resulthtml = resulthtml + "<b>Name:</b>
      <a href='#' onclick = 'showRestaurant(" + i + ")'>" +
      record.attributes["NAME"] + "</a><Br>";
    //display the reating
    resulthtml = resulthtml + "<b>Rating:</b> " +
      record.attributes["RATING"];
    //create a place holder for each review to be populated later
    resulthtml = resulthtml + "<div id = 'review" +
      record.attributes["OBJECTID"] + "'></div>";
    //create a place holder for each attachment picture to be
    populated later
    resulthtml = resulthtml + "<div id = 'picture" +
      record.attributes["OBJECTID"] + "'></div>";
    ```

2. We will need to add a call to a new `AddPictures` function right after `AddReviews` passes the `results` query because we are going to use it:

    ```
    document.getElementById("myresults").innerHTML =
      resulthtml;
          }
    AddReviews(results);
    AddPictures(results);
    }
    ```

3. Next, we create the AddPictures function as follows. This looks similar to the AddReviews function. Loop through the results and prepare the function to query the attachments. There is only one line to be added: the queryAttachmentInfos function. When the attachment query completes, we want it to call the PicturesQueryComplete function that we will add next:

```
...
functionAddPictures(results)
{
  varresultCount = results.features.length;
  for (vari = 0; i<resultCount; i++)
  {
    //for each single feature or record in the result
    var record = results.features[i];
    // Attachment code goes here
    lyr_foodanddrinks.queryAttachmentInfos
       ([record.attributes["OBJECTID"]], PicturesQueryComplete);

  }
}
...
```

4. Finally, we write PicturesQueryComplete. This will receive an array of pictures. We are only interested in the first picture. We will pick it up and create an img HTML element and place it in the corresponding div element by its object ID as shown in the following code. Note that we have used the URL property in the attachment to show the picture. We have resized the picture's width and height to scale it properly in the results panel:

```
functionPicturesQueryComplete(pictures)
{
  //in case of no pictures quit.
  if (pictures.length == 0) return;

  //get the first picture
  var p = pictures[0];

  //set it to its place holder
  document.getElementById("picture" + p.objectId).innerHTML =
    "<imgsrc = '" + p.url + "' width = '200px' height =
    '130px'>";
}
```

Save your file and test it by querying `Fern Diner`. Your application should now display pictures of the restaurants. Take a look at our latest work in the following screenshot:

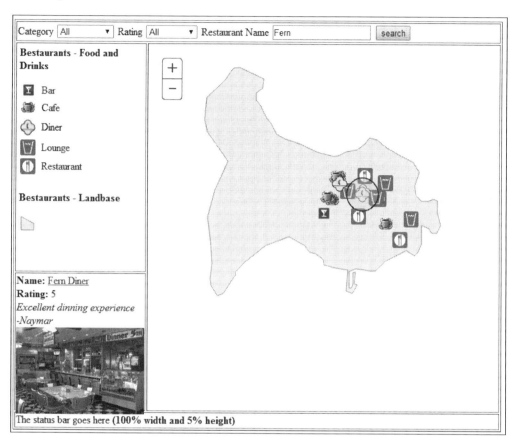

You may find the latest code at `2955OT_04_Files\Code\bestaurants03_pictures.html`.

Mobile integration

Smart phones are becoming a gadget that almost every person has. This has caused businesses to work harder to make their applications and technologies run on mobile. Having the GPS integrated in mobile devices has also boosted the need for Geographic Information Systems (GIS) applications for mobiles. This is why mobile integration of applications is crucial especially with our Bestaurants project, since tourists will be browsing Bestaurants from their mobile most of the time.

The fact that we designed and coded our ArcGIS Web application in JavaScript API makes it easier for us to view it on mobile devices. JavaScript is supported on mobile devices and can be rendered nicely on small handheld devices.

Testing the website on mobile devices

It is important to note that this application was developed to be accessed by both web and mobile users. We will add a small setting that allows us to access the application using mobile devices. To test our website on mobile devices, first, both our web server and the mobile device should connect to the same network. Second, we will need the IP address instead of the machine name. Of course, we will need to add one small tag in our HTML page that will allow our application to be viewed and scaled nicely on mobile devices. Follow these steps to allow running your application on mobile devices:

1. Edit `mybestaurants.html` and add the `viewport` tag at the beginning of the page. This will help render the page in mobile devices:

```
<html>
  <head>
    <meta name="viewport" content="initial-scale=1, maximum-
      scale=1,user-scalable=no"/>
    <title>Bestaurants Web Application</title>
    <linkrel="stylesheet" href="arcgisjs/esri.css">
    <scriptsrc="arcgisjs/3.10/init.js"></script>
```

2. Save `mybestaurants.html` and close it.

3. Get the IP address of your machine by typing the `IPconfig` command in the command prompt. Mine is `192.168.1.2`.

4. We have to enable the Windows Firewall to allow access to port `6080`. This is the port our services are running on. Type `wf.msc` in the run dialog box to open the Windows Firewall options.

5. Right-click on **Inbound Rule** and select **New Role**.

6. In the **Rule Type** dialog box, select **Port**, and click on **Next**.

7. Go to **TCP | Specific Local Port** and then enter `6080` and click on **Next** as shown in the following screenshot:

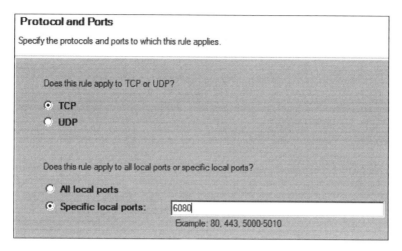

8. Select **All the connection** and click on **Next**.

9. Keep all the options checked (**Domain | Private and Public**) and click on **Next**.

10. Type `ArcGIS for Server Port` in the name and create the rule by clicking on **Finish**.

11. Now that the connections are open, we can safely browse our web application. Open the browser on your mobile device and type in the link `http://192.168.1.2/mybestaurants.html`. Make sure you are connected to the same Wi-Fi network your `arcgismachine` is connected to (`http://192.168.1.2/mybestaurants.html`).

You should see your application and be able to browse it similar to the Web.

GPS integration

By using the satellites, the **Global Position System (GPS)** allows a devices location to be identified. Most mobile devices have a GPS device integrated inside them. Using GPS, users can define their unique locations throughout the world with few meters resolution and can define their (latitude, and longitude) information. We can add some small script in our Bestaurants application to get the latitude and longitude of the device that is currently browsing the application. We will use the built-in navigator object in the browser to achieve that.

Follow these steps to add the GPS integration:

1. Edit the `mybestaurants.html` file and add the following code before the `startup` function:

```
//Get GPS, save them in these variables for later use
varcurrentlat;
varcurrentlong;
if (navigator.geolocation)
{
  navigator.geolocation.getCurrentPosition(showPosition);
}
else
{
  alert( "Geolocation is not supported by this browser.")
}
functionshowPosition(position)
{
  //save the position for later use
  currentlat = position.coords.latitude;
  currentlong = position.coords.longitude;
}
```

2. Save and run the code. You will be prompted with the following message by the browser. Click on **Allow** to allow the navigator to find your location. If you are running the application from a computer, the navigator will use the Wi-Fi network to determine the nearest location, which is not very accurate. If you are running the application from a mobile, the navigator will use the GPS device in your mobile to find the exact location. In short, your location is approximated by using either GPS, which uses satellites and knows your location within a few meters, Wi-Fi, which uses the location of the nearby Wi-Fi networks, or the cell tower, which uses the connection to a cellular network that can be accurate up to a few thousand meters. The location can also be improved with an accelerometer, compass, gyroscope, or barometer in your phone. This was taken from the official Google support (`https://support.google.com/gmm/answer/2839911?hl=en`).

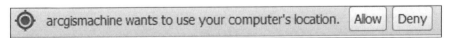

3. Since the GPS coordinates is a point, and we have added a point element before, use the same code or just type in the following function named showGPSLocation. Note that I have hardcoded fake coordinates to show the coordinates. The reason is that unless you are *in* Belize, you cannot actually see this point. The GPS location will basically add a point to your current location:

```
functionshowGPSLocation()
{
  //this is a fake coordinates, since you will not be in Belize
uncomment this if you are in fact in Belize
  currentlat = -88.21;
  currentlong =  17.50;
  var symbol;
  //mark up symbol are for points.
  symbol = new esri.symbol.SimpleMarkerSymbol();
  //set the size
  symbol.setSize(50);
  //and the color (purple) and transparency of 50%
  (0.5)symbol.setColor(new dojo.Color([255,0,255,0.5]));
  //create a graphic object
  var graphic = new esri.Graphic
  (
    // Point coordinates are the gps coordinates, create a point
    newesri.geometry.Point(currentlat, currentlong, map.
spatialReference),//the symbol of the point
symbol
  );

  map.graphics.clear();
  map.graphics.add(graphic);
}
```

4. Finally, we will add a button to show the GPS location in our toolbar that calls the showGPSLocation function as shown in the following code snippet:

```
Restaurant Name <input type = 'text' id = 'txtq'>
  <input type = 'button' value = 'search' onclick =
  'executequery()'>
  <input type = 'button' value = 'GPS' onclick =
    'showGPSLocation()'>
  </td>
</tr>
...
```

5. Save and run `mybestaurants.html` and search for `Faber`. You should get the following screen as the final result:

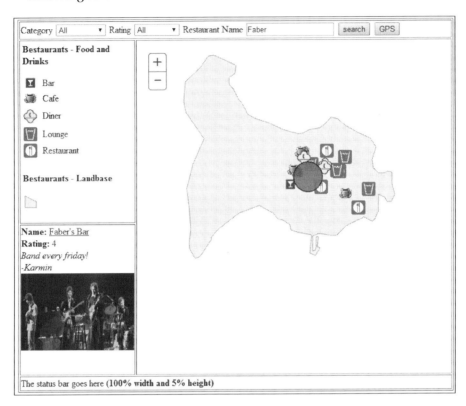

> You can find the final application code with the GPS integration at `29550T_04_Files\Code\bestaurants04_withGPS.html`.

Summary

In this chapter, we injected the Bestaurants web application with rich features. We learned how to perform relationship queries and used them to view the names and reviews of the people who reviewed the restaurants. We then used the same approach to fetch the pictures of the restaurants that were stored as attachments in the feature layer and displayed them on the results. This made the web application more friendly and appealing to the users. We have finally ported the application fully to the mobile by adding the necessary code and enabling the ArcGIS for Server port so that mobile devices can use the service over the Wi-Fi network.

In the next and final chapter, you will learn how to edit feature layers to allow the users to add their own reviews and upload pictures. Editing requires special license of ArcGIS for Server in addition with an enterprise geodatabase. It can also be achieved with ArcGIS Online as we will see in *Appendix, Restaurants on ArcGIS Online*. Before moving to the next chapter, make sure to grab my book *Learning ArcGIS Geodatabases*, published by *Packt Publishing*, and read the last chapter to learn how to fully set up and configure an enterprise geodatabase using Microsoft SQL Server Express.

5
Posting Reviews, Ratings, and Photos

In the previous chapter, we learned to query related data that helped us add more rich content to our Bestaurants web application. Up until now, the website was read-only, so we could search and navigate the map, see pictures of restaurants, and read existing reviews and ratings. However, we didn't update or edit any data. That is because editing requires us to modify some settings in both the service and our code before we can allow the user to make any changes.

In this chapter, we will learn how to perform editing on services by adding three features: posting reviews, ratings, and uploading pictures for the restaurant.

Configuring enterprise Geodatabase

Unfortunately, editing requires some more configurations to be done, and the current service we have already published in *Chapter 1*, *The Bestaurants Project*, wouldn't do the trick. The reason is that the service is using a local database file; however, editing GIS data on the Web requires either an enterprise database running on a database management server such as the SQL server, or Oracle, or an ArcGIS Online feature service. Setting up the enterprise geodatabase server is out of the scope of this book. However, you can grab my book *Learning ArcGIS Geodatabase*, published by *Packt Publishing*, and walk through the step-by-step full guide to set up your own enterprise geodatabase with Microsoft SQL Server Express. If you have an existing enterprise geodatabase server, you can use it. I will be using SQL Server Express 2012 SP1.

Connecting to the Geodatabase

First, we need to establish a connection to the enterprise server. For that we will use a username that has full editing capabilities. I will be using the **system administrator (SA)** user `sa` for the SQL server.

 Note that the SA user has full access to the database; we have used it in this book for simplicity to avoid assigning privileges. In an ideal situation, you would create a user and assign him the correct permissions to read or write into the subject tables. My book, *Learning ArcGIS Geodatabase*, published by *Packt Publishing*, addresses all these issues thoroughly.

Follow these steps to establish a connection to your enterprise geodatabase:

1. Open **ArcCatalog** and expand **Database Connections** in the **Catalog Tree** panel.

2. Double-click on **Add Database Connection**.

3. In the **Database Platform** option select **SQL Server** (or your database provider).

4. Type the name of the server hosting the database; in my case, it is the same server `arcgismachine`.

5. Select **Database authentication** in **Authentication Type** and provide the database credentials for the `sa` user or any user who has administrator privileges on the database. You can use the `SDE` user as well.

6. Select your **Database** from the drop-down list and click on **OK** as shown in the following screenshot:

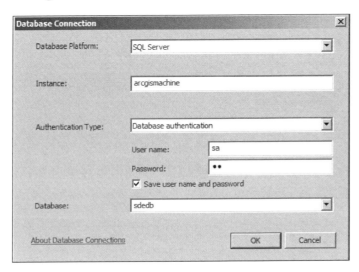

7. Rename the connection to `sa@arcgismachine.sde`. We are going to reference this later in the chapter. Don't close ArcCatalog yet, as we will be needing it.

 You can learn more about ArcGIS database connections and how to create them against different databases from the link `http://qr.net/arcgisdb`.

Copying Bestaurants' data to the server

Now that we have our connection ready, we need to copy the Bestaurants data into our new database. Follow these steps:

1. From **Catalog Tree**, right-click on the **Folder connection** and select **Connect to Folder**. Browse to `C:\2955OT`, the folder we created in the first chapter, and click **OK**. This will allow us to access our Bestaurants data.

2. From **Folder Connection**, expand `C:\2955OT` and browse to `2955OT_01_Files\Bestaurants.gdb`.

3. Click on **Bestaurants.gdb**, use the *Shift* key to select **Belize_Landbase** and **Food_and_Drinks**. Then right-click and select **Copy** as shown in the following screenshot:

4. Double-click on the `ags@arcgismachine.sde` connection to open it. Right-click on the connection and select **Paste**. You will be prompted with the following dialog box that will show you what will be copied. Note that related data was also imported. This will paste the data to our new database.

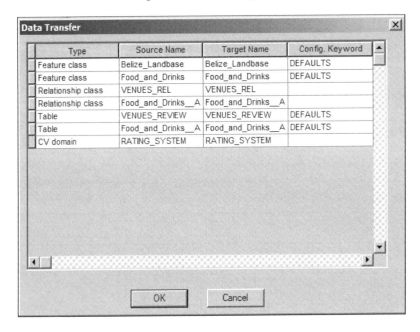

5. After the copying is completed, close **ArcCatalog**.

Publishing feature service

Our old service won't work in this chapter; the reason is that it was pointing to a local database which does not support editing on ArcGIS for Server. That is why we migrated our Restaurants data to the enterprise geodatabase. It is time to publish a brand new service; it will look the same but will just behave differently. First, we need to open our `Belize.mxd` map document and point our new database. Second, we will register the database with ArcGIS for Server; finally, we will publish the service.

Setting the Source to the Enterprise Geodatabase

In order to publish the new service, we have to first create a map document which points to the enterprise geodatabase. Follow these steps to do so:

1. Browse to and open 2955OT_05_Files\Belize.mxd with ArcMap. You can simply double-click on the file.

2. Next, we set the source of our layers from the **Table of Contents** in **ArcMap**. Click on **List by Source** as shown in this screenshot:

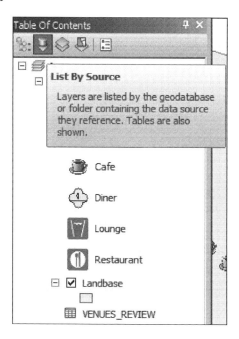

3. Double-click on the **Food_and_Drinks** layer to open the Layer properties.

4. In the **Layer Properties** window, click on **Set Data Source**.

5. From the **Data Source** dialog, browse to the **sa@arcgismachine.sde** connection and select the **sdedb.DBO.Food_and_Drinks** object, and then click on **Add** as illustrated in this screenshot:

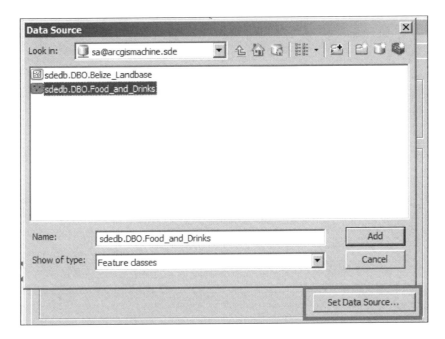

6. Click **OK** to apply the changes.

7. Do the same for the rest of the objects, **Landbase** and **VENUES_REVIEW**, in your map selecting the matching objects in the destination connection.

8. The final source list should look like the following, with nothing pointing to the local data. Keep **ArcMap** open for the next step.

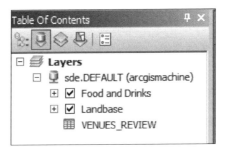

You can also modify the data sources in an ArcMap document using ArcCatalog.

In ArcCatalog, navigate to the map document in **Catalog Tree**, right-click on the map document, and choose the **Set Data Sources** option from the pop-up menu. Using this allows you to set the data source for individual and/or all layers at one time.

Publishing the map document

Now that we have our map document ready, it is time for us to publish it. However, we still need to perform one more step, which is database registration. This step will cause the data to persist in the server, which makes it ready for editing. Follow these steps to publish the map document:

1. From the **File** menu, point to **Share As** and click on **Service**.

2. Select **Overwrite an existing service**, because we want to replace our old Bestaurants service from *Chapter 1*, *The Bestaurants Project*. Click on **Next**.

3. Select the **Bestaurants** service and click on **Continue**.

4. From the **Service Editor** window, click on **Capabilities**.

5. Check the **Feature Access** capability to enable editing on this service as shown in the following screenshot:

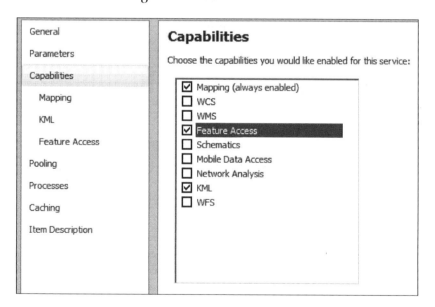

6. Click on **Analyze**. This will show an error that we have to fix. The error is **Feature service requires a registered database**. This error can be solved by right-clicking on it and selecting **Show Data Store Registration Page**, as shown in the following screenshot:

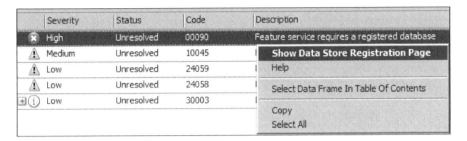

7. In the **Data Store** window, click on the plus sign to add a new database.

8. In the **Register Database** window, enter in `Bestaurants` in the **Name** textbox.

9. Click on **Import** and select the **sa@arcgismachine** connection. Make sure the **Same as publisher database connection** option is checked as shown in the following screenshot:

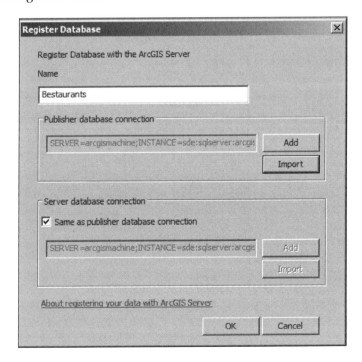

10. Click on **OK** in the **Register Database** window and the **Data Store** window.

11. Click on **Analyse** again; this time you shouldn't get any errors. Go ahead and **Publish** your service.

12. Close **ArcMap**.

> You can read more about registering databases at:
> `http://qr.net/registerdb`.

Testing the web application with the new service

We have updated our Bestaurants service, but it should work fine so far. Just make sure that you run your application under `http://arcgismachine/mybestaurants.html`.

> You can find the latest code at `2955OT_05_Files\Code\bestaurants01_beforeediting.html`. Copy it to `c:\inetpub\wwwroot` and rename it accordingly.

Adding ArcGIS's editing capabilities

Currently, the food and drinks layer is being fetched as a read-only map service located at the URL: `http://arcgismachine:6080/arcgis/rest/services/Bestaurants/MapServer/0`. The only difference is that it points to the enterprise geodatabase. You can see the following code in `mybestaurants.html` which confirms that:

```
//load the food and drinks layer into an object
lyr_foodanddrinks = new esri.layers.FeatureLayer
  ("http://arcgismachine:6080/arcgis/rest/
  services/Bestaurants/MapServer/0", { outFields: ["*"] }
);
```

We won't be able to edit `MapServerlayer`, we have to use `FeatureServer`. We will show how to change this in the next section.

Adding or updating records in a service with ArcGIS JavaScript API is simple. We only need to use the `applyEdits` method on the `FeatureLayer` object. This method accepts a record and some parameters for the response; what we are interested in is to insert a record. The following code shows how to prepare a record with three fields for this function:

```
varnewrecord =
{
attributes:
  {
     FIELD1: VALUE1,
     FIELD2: VALUE2,
     FIELD3: VALUE3
  }
};
```

For instance, if I want to create a new record that has rating and review, I populate them as follows:

```
varnewrecord =
  {
  attributes:
  {
     REVIEW: "This is a sample review",
     RATING: 2,
     USER: "Hussein"
  }
};
```

And to add this record, we simply call `applyEdits` on the corresponding layer and pass the `newrecord` object as shown in the following code snippet:

```
var layer = new esri.layers.FeatureLayer("URL");
layer.applyEdits([newrecord], null, null, null, null);
```

Posting reviews and ratings

The first thing we have to do is to point our food and drinks layer to its feature server instead of the map server to allow editing. This can be achieved by using the following URL instead. Simply replace `MapServer` with `FeatureServer`:

```
http://arcgismachine:6080/arcgis/rest/services/Bestaurants/
FeatureServer/0
```

Follow these steps to perform the first change towards editing our service:

1. Edit `mybestaurants.html`. Find the food and drinks layer initialization and point it to the feature service instead using the following code snippet:

```
//load the food and drinks layer into an object
lyr_foodanddrinks = new
  esri.layers.FeatureLayer
  ("http://arcgismachine:6080/arcgis/rest/services
  /Bestaurants/FeatureServer/0", { outFields: ["*"] }
);
```

2. As we have seen in *Chapter 4, Rich Content and Mobile Integration,* the review and rating fields can be found in the **VENUES_REVIEW** table. So we can add a single record that has a review and a rating, and send it to the service. However, we need to prepare the necessary controls that will eventually populate and add a record to the reviews table. Let's modify the `ShowResults` function of our query so that each restaurant shows two textboxes: one for review and one for the rating. We will also add a button so that we can call the `addnewreview()` function that will add the review. Each control will be identified with the object ID of the restaurant as shown in the following code:

```
//display the reating
resulthtml = resulthtml + "<b>Rating:</b> " +
  record.attributes["RATING"];
//create a place holder for each review to be populated later
resulthtml = resulthtml + "<div id = 'review" +
  record.attributes["OBJECTID"] + "'></div>";
//create a place holder for each attachment picture to be
populated later
resulthtml = resulthtml + "<div id = 'picture" +
  record.attributes["OBJECTID"] + "'></div>";
//create text box for the review marked with the objectid
resulthtml = resulthtml + "<br>Review: <input type = 'text' id
  = 'txtreview" + record.attributes["OBJECTID"] + "'>";

//another one for the rating.
resulthtml = resulthtml + "<br>Rating: <input type = 'text' id
  = 'txtrating" + record.attributes["OBJECTID"] + "'>";

//and a button to call the function addnewreview
resulthtml = resulthtml + "<br><input type = 'button' value =
  'Add' onclick = 'addnewreview(" +
  record.attributes["OBJECTID"] + ")'>";
```

3. Now, we need to write the `addnewreview` function. This function accepts an object ID and adds a record matching that object to the reviews table. I have placed the three empty variables: object ID, review, and rating, and prepared the template to write a new record. I also created a feature layer of our **VENUES_REVIEW** table; see *Chapter 4, Rich Content and Mobile Integration*, to see how I got the URL:

```
functionaddnewreview(oid)
{
  varobjectid;
  var review;
  var rating;
  varnewReview =
  {
    attributes:
    {
      VENUE_OBJECTID: objectid,
      REVIEW: review,
      RATING: rating
    }
  };
  //open the review table,as we seen in chapter 4 it has an id of
2
  varreviewtable = new esri.layers.FeatureLayer
  ("http://arcgismachine:6080/arcgis/rest/services
  /Bestaurants/FeatureServer/2");
  //apply edits and pass the review record
  reviewtable.applyEdits([newReview], null, null, null, null);
}
```

4. You might have guessed how to obtain the review, rating, and object ID. The object ID is passed, so that is easy. The review can be obtained by searching for `txtreview + objectid`. A similar search can be used for rating. Let's also add a message to see if things went fine:

```
functionaddnewreview(oid)
{
  varobjectid = oid;
  var review  =document.getElementById('txtreview' +
    oid).value;
```

```
var rating = document.getElementById('txtrating' +
  oid).value;
varnewReview =
{
  attributes:
  {
    VENUE_OBJECTID: objectid,
    REVIEW: review,
    RATING: rating
  }
};
//open the review table,as we seen in chapter 4 it has an id of
2
varreviewtable = new esri.layers.FeatureLayer
  ("http://arcgismachine:6080/arcgis/rest/services
  /Bestaurants/FeatureServer/2");
//apply edits and pass the review record
reviewtable.applyEdits([newReview], null, null,
  null, null);
alert("Review has been added");
}
```

5. You can also add the user to your record in a similar way:

```
varnewReview =
{
  attributes:
  {
    OBJECTID: objectid,
    REVIEW: review,
    USER_ : "Hussein"
    RATING: rating
  }
};
```

6. It is time for us to save and run our new application. Do a search on `Fern`, then write a review, add a rating, and then click on **Add**. This should add a record to **Fern Diner**. You can always check if your record is added or not from **ArcCatalog**. This can be seen in the following screenshot:

> You can find the latest code at `2955OT_05_Files\Code\bestaurants02_addreviews.html`.

Uploading pictures

Uploading attachments to a service can be achieved by calling the `addAttachment` method on the feature layer object. However, we have to make some changes in our `ShowResults` function to ask the user to browse for a file. For that, we will need to use the file's HTML object, but we have to encapsulate it in a form tagged by the object ID of the restaurant we want to upload the pictures for. The file object should be named `attachment` so that the `addAttachment` method can find it. Follow these steps to add the upload pictures' logic:

1. Edit the `mybestaurants.html` file and add the following code to your `ShowResults` function:

    ```
    //browse for a picture for this restaurant
    ```

```
resulthtml = resulthtml + "<form id = 'frm" +
  record.attributes["OBJECTID"] + "'><input type =
  'file' name = 'attachment'/></form>";
//and a button to call the function addnewreview
resulthtml = resulthtml + "<br>
  <input type = 'button' value = 'Add' onclick =
  'addnewreview(" + record.attributes["OBJECTID"] + ")'>";
//new line
resulthtml = resulthtml + "<br><br>";
```

2. We will make it so that when the user clicks on **Add**, the attachment is also added along with the review for simplicity. The `AddAttachment` function takes the object ID of the restaurant which you want to upload the picture to, and a form HTML element which contains the file element named attachment:

```
functionaddnewreview(oid)
{
  varobjectid = oid;
  var review  =  document.getElementById('txtreview' +
    oid).value;
  var rating = document.getElementById('txtrating' +
    oid).value;
  varnewReview =
  {
    attributes:
    {
      VENUE_OBJECTID: objectid,
      USER_: "Hussein",
      REVIEW: review,
      RATING: rating
    }
  };
  //open the review table,as we seen in chapter 4 it has an id of
2
  varreviewtable = new esri.layers.FeatureLayer
  ("http://arcgismachine:6080/arcgis/rest/services
    /Bestaurants/FeatureServer/2");
  //apply edits and pass the review record
  reviewtable.applyEdits
    ([newReview], null, null, null, null);
//add attachment
```

```
lyr_foodanddrinks.addAttachment(oid,
    document.getElementById("frm" + oid) , null, null);

alert("Review and picture has been added");
}
```

3. Save and run the code. Search for **Haulze Restaurant**. This one doesn't have an attachment, so go ahead, write a review, and upload a picture. Run the query again and you should see your picture. This is shown in the following screenshot:

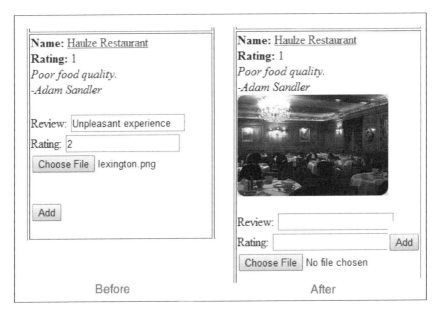

Before   After

 The final code can be found at 29550T_05_Files\Code\ bestaurants03_uploadpicture.html.

The final touches

This is where we add some web enhancements to the application, things that you as a web developer can do. We will update the status bar, make part of the page scrollable, change the rating into star icons, and do some fine-tuning of the interface. I have already implemented these changes in the final version of the application, which can be found at `2955OT_05_Files\Code\bestaurantsfinal.html`. These changes don't have anything to do with ArcGIS development; it is pure HTML and JavaScript. The final application should look as shown in the following screenshot:

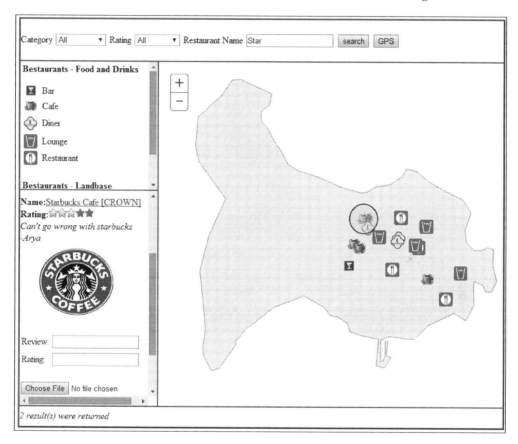

Summary

In this chapter, we have put the final touches to the Bestaurants ArcGIS web application by adding rating, reviews, and uploading pictures to the ArcGIS service. We have learned that editing can only be done for the feature services on the data hosted on enterprise geodatabases – that is why we had to set up our own. We have copied the data to a new server, and modified the source document to point to that server. Then we republished the service with feature-access capability to enable editing. We finally added the necessary JavaScript API code to write reviews and upload pictures to the website. With these features, we have completed the Bestaurants project requirements.

This is the end of this book but it is only the beginning of great potential applications that you will be developing using the skill set you acquired in the course of this journey.

You can now be confident in pursuing more advanced ArcGIS JavaScript APIs from the Esri website (`resources.arcgis.com`) which is a good place to start. There are hundreds of methods and functions in the API. However, keep in mind that you only need to learn what you really need and require. We have managed to complete an entire website with a handful of APIs. Take the next project, analyze the requirements, see what APIs you need, and learn them. That is my advice. My inbox is always ready for suggestions and thoughts, and of course, questions.

Bestaurants on ArcGIS Online

By the end of the last chapter, we managed to wrap up and complete our ArcGIS web application using ArcGIS for Server as the backend server and JavaScript API as the client-side application. Esri has invested a lot in a new technology to completely migrate the ArcGIS technology to the web platform, which they call ArcGIS Online. With this technology, you can author your maps to your ArcGIS online account and consume it via various built-in template applications. You can also customize your own application to utilize an ArcGIS online map.

In this Appendix, we will learn how to create an ArcGIS online account, upload our Bestaurants data to create a map on our account, and then finally, we will use the ArcGIS JavaScript API to consume the online Bestaurants map.

Setting up ArcGIS Online account

To start working on ArcGIS Online, you should have an Esri global account. The global account allows you to have access to all Esri services and products including ArcGIS Online. You can use it to write posts in the Esri forums or post ideas in the ideas portal (`ideas.arcgis.com`). So first, we will create the global account. Follow these steps to do so:

1. Open your browser and visit the following address:

   `https://www.arcgis.com/home/createaccount.html`

2. In the **Create Your Public Account** page, fill in your information. The **Username** is your ID and it will show everywhere within Esri websites and services.

3. Click on **Review and Accept the Terms of Use** and click on **I Accept**.

4. Click on **Create My Account** and activate your account when necessary as shown in the following screenshot:

Publishing an ArcGIS Online Map

You have created your ArcGIS Online account; this account gives you limited access to www.ArcGIS.com. You can still do a lot of things with the free account, such as create, share, and utilize maps from your local web server.

You can check out the additional features and pricing by subscribing to ArcGIS Online at:

http://www.esri.com/software/arcgis/arcgisonline/
purchase

In this section, we will create our first ArcGIS Online map. To do that, we will upload our Bestaurants data. I have converted the Bestaurants database to a friendly format supported by ArcGIS Online. It is available in the supporting files that are provided for this Appendix. Before you continue, download the supporting file for this Appendix from the folder labeled 29550T_AA and copy them on to your local drive. Follow these steps to create your first ArcGIS Online map:

1. After you log in from the main menu, click on **My Content**. This is where all your maps can be found. You can use the same place to create and share your maps with the public.

2. From the folders section on the left, click on the folder under your name. Mine is **EdmondDantes (Home)**.

3. Click on **Create Map** to create your first online map. If you are prompted with a dialog box, click on **Yes Open the Map**. This is illustrated in the following screenshot:

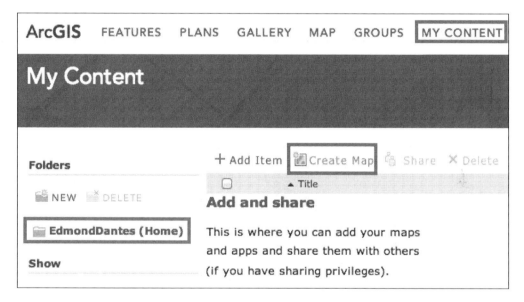

4. You will be directed to a new page; they will provide you with a map of the world data. We are interested in Belize; so, we have to zoom in there. In the top-right search box, enter Belize and hit *Enter*, this will zoom in to the **Belize** country.

5. Next, we will add our Bestaurants data. From the **Add** menu, click on **Add Layer** from **File** and then browse the data, which you can find at 29550T_AA\ Shapefiles\Bestaurants.zip, and then click on **Import Layer**. This is illustrated in the following screenshot:

6. Note that our data has been added to the map and marked as red dots. That is because ArcGIS online doesn't know what icons we want to use for our data. Don't worry, we can change this. Also, you can find some basic tools in the viewer provided by ArcGIS Online, such as the identify and measure tools. Take a few moments to test these built-in tools.

7. Now, we will label our restaurants so that they are named on the map. From the **Contents** panel, click on the small arrow next to the Bestaurants layer and select **Create Labels**. Make sure that the **Name** field is selected. Now, click on **OK**.

8. To change the symbols based on the type of the restaurant, click on the small arrow next to the Bestaurants layer and select **Change Symbols**.

9. In the **Change Symbols** panel, select **Unique Symbols** from the drop-down list, then select the field you want to base your symbols on. This will be our **Type** field.

10. Use the **Options** menu to **Change All Symbols** to a diamond and click on **Apply**. You should see a map similar to the following screenshot:

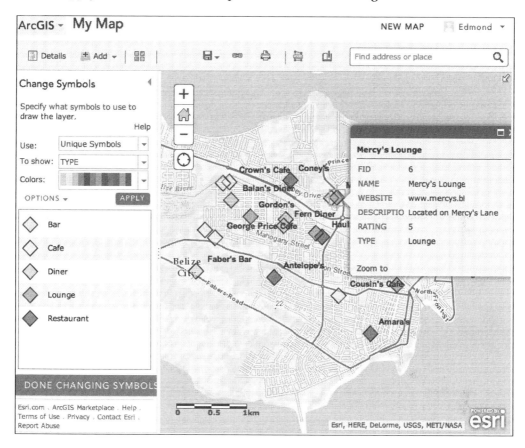

11. We are ready to save our map. Click on the **Save** button and name it **Bestaurants**, enter a tag line, a summary, and click on **Save Map**. This map is now private, so only you can see it, but we still need to share it with the public so that everyone can view it, and so that we can use it from the JavaScript API.

12. From the **ArcGIS** menu, go back to **My Content** and click on your folder. You should now see the **Bestaurants** map created, and ready to be shared.

13. Check the Restaurants map, then click on **Share** and check **Everyone (public)**. Click on **OK** to finish as illustrated in the following screenshot:

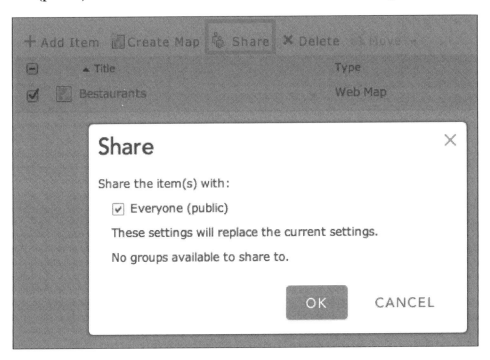

Using online map from the JavaScript API

Although the ArcGIS online map viewer is incredibly easy to use and configure, it is still limited, and doesn't allow us to add our own code and functionality. That is why Esri allowed you to use ArcGIS JavaScript API to extend the functionality of ArcGIS Online so that they can host the data and you work on the application. Luckily, Esri has provided us with the source code of a complete JavaScript API viewer for ArcGIS Online. All you have to do is to add some configurations and you are ready to use it. In this section, we will learn how to connect ArcGIS Online using the JavaScript API viewer.

Each map you create in ArcGIS Online has a unique global map ID; yes, even the one you just created has an ID and we will need this ID to connect to our map. Follow these steps to get your map ID and configure your ArcGIS online viewer:

1. Log in to `www.arcgis.com` and then click on **My Content**.

2. Click on Bestaurants map to open it.

3. Take a look at the address bar. You will see a link similar to `http://www.arcgis.com/home/item.html?id=8a8ada9b1a794` `39eb8a2c4d929b8d74d`. That is your map ID after the `id=`, mine is `8a8ada9b1a79439eb8a2c4d929b8d74d`; keep yours in a safe place since we will be using it.

4. Now, we will use the ArcGIS Online JavaScript Viewer to point to our Bestaurants map. You can find the viewer at `2955OT_AA\OnlineViewer`. Copy the `OnlineViewer` folder to `c:\inetpub\wwwroot`.

5. Using windows explorer, browse `C:\inetpub\wwwroot\OnlineViewer\` `config`. This is where the configuration of the web viewer is located.

6. Using `Notepad++`, edit the `defaults.js` file and add your map ID in the `Webmap` key as shown in the following screenshot:

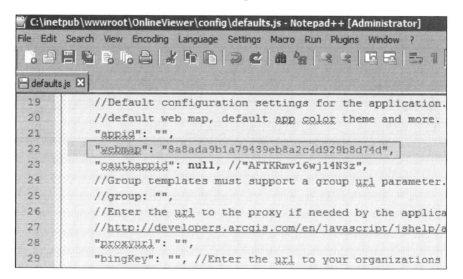

Believe it or not, that is it!

7. Browse your new web application at `http://arcgismachine/` `OnlineViewer`. Take some time to explore the rich tools the viewer provides you with. Its source code can be found at `C:\inetpub\wwwroot\` `OnlineViewer\index.html`.

8. Edit the file and use your JavaScript API skills and tools you have acquired in this book to add your own functionalities to it as shown in the following screenshot:

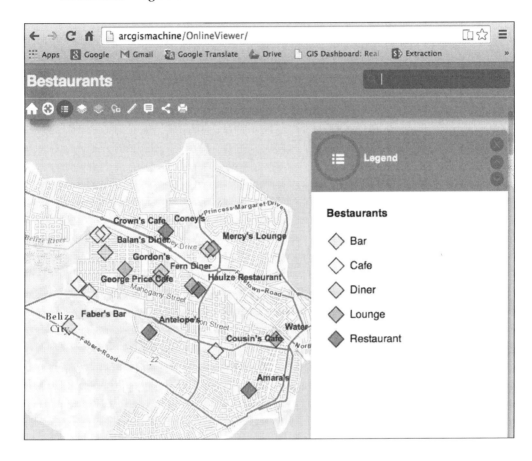

Summary

In this Appendix, we have learned how to create an ArcGIS Online account and use it to author an online map hosted on Esri servers. We have uploaded our Bestaurants data to the map and changed the labels and symbols. Then, we have used the ArcGIS Online JavaScript API to consume the ArcGIS Online map by pointing the configuration to the online map. Although we couldn't do the post review features, since ArcGIS Online free account doesn't have the editing feature, we still managed to recreate the Bestaurants website from scratch without any programming.

ArcGIS Online can give you a great out-of-the-box experience when it comes to building websites, especially if your website is simple, straightforward, and has clear functionalities. However, with ArcGIS for Server, you have the absolute freedom when it comes to customizations. You can build the entire website from scratch and, with the power of the JavaScript API, you can do a lot. ArcGIS Online is a new product. It is being enhanced and maintained on a daily basis. It is up to you which product you want to go with. Maybe in the future, when ArcGIS Online matures more, we will write a dedicated book for it.

This was a great journey; I hope you have benefited from the Bestaurants project. Feel free to contact me with any questions or suggestions.

Index

E

F

G

H

I

J

L

M

N

name
restaurants, displaying by 62
restaurants, searching by 61
Notepad++
URL 29

O

ObjectID 74

P

port 34
project statement, Bestaurants 10
published service, Bestaurants
testing 25, 26
publishing service
in ArcGIS for Server 22-25

Q

query results
displaying 62-66

R

rating
filtering by 59, 60
relationship query example 75-77
relationships
about 73
foreign key 74
primary key 74
restaurants
displaying, by name 61
identifying 52-54
map highlighting, by results
interaction 67-70
query results, displaying 62-66
searching, by name 61

rich content, restaurants
pictures, displaying 83, 84
reviews, displaying 79-82
working with 79
results
interacting with, to highlight map 67-69

S

server
Bestaurants, data copying to 95, 96
service
publishing, in ArcGIS for Server 22-24
Silverlight 15
source
adding, to enterprise geodatabase 97-99
Structured Query Language (SQL) 17
system administrator (SA) 94

U

user interface (UI) 32

W

web server
IIS, installing 30-32
setting up 30
testing 33
web service 8
website
testing, on mobile devices 86, 87
WKID (Well-Known-ID) 42

Thank you for buying
Building Web Applications with ArcGIS

About Packt Publishing

Packt, pronounced 'packed', published its first book "*Mastering phpMyAdmin for Effective MySQL Management*" in April 2004 and subsequently continued to specialize in publishing highly focused books on specific technologies and solutions.

Our books and publications share the experiences of your fellow IT professionals in adapting and customizing today's systems, applications, and frameworks. Our solution based books give you the knowledge and power to customize the software and technologies you're using to get the job done. Packt books are more specific and less general than the IT books you have seen in the past. Our unique business model allows us to bring you more focused information, giving you more of what you need to know, and less of what you don't.

Packt is a modern, yet unique publishing company, which focuses on producing quality, cutting-edge books for communities of developers, administrators, and newbies alike. For more information, please visit our website: www.packtpub.com.

Writing for Packt

We welcome all inquiries from people who are interested in authoring. Book proposals should be sent to author@packtpub.com. If your book idea is still at an early stage and you would like to discuss it first before writing a formal book proposal, contact us; one of our commissioning editors will get in touch with you.

We're not just looking for published authors; if you have strong technical skills but no writing experience, our experienced editors can help you develop a writing career, or simply get some additional reward for your expertise.

Building Web and Mobile ArcGIS Server Applications with JavaScript

ISBN: 978-1-84969-796-5   Paperback: 274 pages

Master the ArcGIS API for JavaScript, and build exciting, custom web and mobile GIS applications with the ArcGIS Server

1. Develop ArcGIS Server applications with JavaScript, both for traditional web browsers as well as the mobile platform.

2. Acquire in-demand GIS skills sought by many employers.

3. Step-by-step instructions, examples, and hands-on practice designed to help you learn the key features and design considerations for building custom ArcGIS Server applications.

Administering ArcGIS for Server

ISBN: 978-1-78217-736-4   Paperback: 246 pages

Installing and configuring ArcGIS for Server to publish, optimize, and secure GIS services

1. Configure ArcGIS for Server to achieve maximum performance and response time.

2. Understand the product mechanics to build up good troubleshooting skills.

3. Filled with practical exercises, examples, and code snippets to help facilitate your learning.

Please check **www.PacktPub.com** for information on our titles

Made in the USA
Lexington, KY
30 March 2015